Egalitarians
and the
Bible

An Exposition and Defense of the
Egalitarian View

by Francis H. Geis II

Christians for Biblical Equality
cbeinternational.org

Egalitarians and the Bible: An Exposition and Defense of the Egalitarian View

© 2011 by Francis H. Geis II

Published by Christians for Biblical Equality
122 W Franklin Ave, Suite 218
Minneapolis, MN 55404
cbeinternational.org

All references to the NIV are to the 2010 revision: THE HOLY BIBLE, NEW INTERNATIONAL VERSION®, NIV® Copyright © 1973, 1978, 1984, 2010 by Biblica, Inc.™ Used by permission. All rights reserved worldwide.

ISBN: 978-0-9778909-5-8 (Print)
ISBN: 978-0-9778909-6-5 (PDF)
ISBN: 978-1-939971-04-3 (e-PUB)
ISBN: 978-1-939971-05-0 (MOBI)

Printed in the United States of America

All rights reserved. No part of this publication may be reproduced, stored in a retrieval system, or transmitted in any form or by any means—for example, electronic, photocopy, recording—without the prior written permission of the publisher. The only exception is brief quotation in printed reviews.

Table of Contents

Preface	5
General and Special Revelation	7
The Necessity of a Written Revelation	14
The New Testament and Ancient Greco-Roman Historians	21
The New Testament Writers as Historians and Theologians	30
Misrepresentations, Corrections, and Proper Interpretation	38
Issues Regarding Interpretation and Application of Scripture	47
Pneumatic-Communal Interpretation of Scripture and Conflict Resolution	58
Bibliography	71
About CBE	77

Preface

A number of well written, scholarly books have already been produced that both explain and defend the egalitarian view on the inspiration, authority and interpretation of Scripture. And so this little booklet, drawing on a number of these same sources, is not intended in any way to replace them. However, in a discussion with some friends, it became clear that there was a need for a series of articles or a small booklet which showed that egalitarians, contrary to frequent charges otherwise, had a very high view of the Bible's inspiration, trustworthiness, and authority. This resource could serve as a ready reference to share with people who really wanted to know and understand how egalitarians really viewed and used the Scriptures. So in response to that discussion and the apparent need, I have produced this booklet.

The first four chapters discuss aspects of Scripture upon which all Evangelical Christians mostly agree, such as the distinction between General and Special Revelation; the necessity of God's revelation through Christ and the Apostles being put down in permanent written form; what we mean and do not mean by terms such as inspiration, inerrancy, and infallibility of Scripture; and the historical reliability of the New Testament writings. This material can be used by any Christian, whether egalitarian or hierarchical-complementarian, to proclaim and defend the Evangelical view of Scripture.

However, the last three chapters concentrate on correcting various misrepresentations of the egalitarian view of Scripture. Among the things discussed in these chapters is the true nature and scope of the *Sola*

Scriptura principle, valid and invalid interpretation of Scripture, and a call for reconciliation and reformation.

As regards myself, the author of this booklet, I am an educated lay minister. I received my B.B.S. at Western Bible College; my B.A. in Arts and Humanities at Colorado Christian College, and spent one year at a Reformed Episcopal seminary, studying the translation and exegesis of the Hebrew Old Testament. I have served in several churches in various capacities, such as a Bible teacher and deacon, as well as being part of various worship teams. I also served as an associate editor of the *Journal of Biblical Equality* from 1988 to 1992. I only mention this for those who might wonder what *credentials* I have for writing this booklet. However, whatever wisdom, knowledge, and skill in teaching I may have has been given to me by the Lord himself. So if I do any boasting, it will be in him whom I truly know as the one who delights in demonstrating steadfast love, justice, and righteousness in all His dealings with us (Jer. 9:23-24). Nevertheless, may he be pleased to bless this labor of love and use it for the good of the church. Amen.

General and Special Revelation

Several years ago, while serving as an alternate teacher for our church's adult Sunday school class, I gave a series of lessons on the origin, transmission, preservation, and translation of the Bible. I am presently working on turning this material into a book that Christians can use in explaining and defending their view of the inspiration, authority, and reliability of the Bible as a whole, and of the New Testament in particular. But seeing a need for it among egalitarians resources, I have decided to address those misconceptions that exist about what Christians believe about the nature and purpose of the Bible, and also to refute the widespread view that egalitarian Christians, such as myself, have a low view of the inspiration, authority, and reliability of Scripture. So, in this first discussion, we will focus on the topic of general and special revelation.

General and Special Revelation Defined

As humans have explored and studied the world around them, they have been impressed with the fact that the universe has an evident origin. It has evident regulatory processes, and an evident functional design. They have also discovered that the universe functions in a rationally accessible way; that there is a strange agreement between the way our minds work and the structure of the world we live in. So they believe that the rationality of human beings and the universe they live in can only be satisfactorily explained by a great mind being behind both. And when they consider the realities of human consciousness and moral conscience, for which Neo-Darwinism has no rationally consistent and coherent explanation, many are convinced that a great rational and moral being is the only explanation for the origin of human capacities for rationality and morality, and not some mindless, amoral, purposeless evolutionary process. Indeed, it was this failure of atheistic naturalism to explain both the rationality of the universe and of the rational, self-consciousness of humanity that led Antony Flew, the great English philosopher and author, to change his view in 2004 regarding God and the origin of the universe, as he clearly states in his book, *There Is A God* (Harper One, 2007).

Furthermore, many astronomers, physicists, and biochemists are, by means of scientific investigation and analysis, confirming that the existence of the present universe, as a fine-tuned environment for the existence and sustenance of intelligent and moral beings like ourselves, cannot be the result of a random, by chance accident.

Roger Penrose, professor of mathematics at Oxford University, has among his areas of expertise the study of the universe shortly after its creation. He was awarded the Wolf Prize for his analytic description of the Big Bang, which forms the basis of all Big Bang cosmology. Penrose finds the laws of nature [fine] tuned for life. The balance of nature's laws is so perfect and so unlikely to have occurred by chance that he avers an intelligent 'Creator' must have chosen them. It is as if we were written into the equations of the universe at its inception or in the words of physicist Paul Davies 'built into the scheme of things in a very basic way.'"[1]

It is this form of revelation through the created universe and through the innate rational and moral consciousness of humanity which causes people to generally recognize a divine creator, ruler and judge. Theologians call this either *general* or *natural revelation*. And it is also recognized as the general rational and moral foundation that has given stability to past human societies, and been the starting point of most ethical systems prior to modern times. However, because of the sinful tendencies of the human heart since the fall (Gen. 3), general revelation is a revelation that people have tended to either ignore or to reinterpret to their own advantage, as St. Paul makes clear in Romans 1:18-23:

> The wrath of God is being revealed from heaven against all the godlessness and wickedness of human beings who suppress the truth by their wickedness, since what may be known about God is plain to them, because God has made it plain to them. For since the creation of the world God's invisible qualities—his eternal power and divine nature—have been clearly seen, being understood from what has been made, so that people are without excuse. For although they knew God, they neither glorified him as God nor gave thanks to him, but their thinking became futile and their foolish hearts were darkened. Although they claimed to be wise, they became fools and exchanged the glory of the immortal God for images made to look like mortal human beings and birds and animals and reptiles (Rom. 1:18-23, TNIV).

Now, when we speak of *special revelation*, we are, of course, speaking of the revelation that God has given to humanity which surpasses that of natural revelation. This revelation of God's nature has been communicated to humanity in various ways and by various agents throughout human history. First, God has been made known through *visions, dreams and wondrous signs*. In both the Old and New Testament times, God has come to various people and then been made known to them through visions, dreams, angelic visitations, and theophanies—*i.e.,* varied audio-visual manifestations of God's actual presence (*cf.* Job 33:12-18; Gen. 28:10-22; 18:1-19:29; Dan. 8:15-27; 10:7-14; Lk. 1:5-20; Acts 1:10-11; Exod. 3:1-6; 14:23-25; 19:16-19; 2 Chron. 7:1-3; Lk. 9:34-36). Secondly, both God's character and will has been made known through *direct verbal communication*. In either an apparently "audible voice" or by a "voice in the head," God spoke directly and personally to various people, who then went on to write down and preserve the prophetic message(s) (*cf.* Num. 12:5-8; 15:22-25; Deut. 18: 14-20; 31:9-13; 2 Kings 17:13-15; Jer. 36:1-7; Hab. 2:1-3; and Amos 3:7-8). Lastly, God has been revealed through the *life, words, and deeds of Jesus Christ, the Word made flesh*, which are faithfully recorded and interpreted in the New Testament writings (*cf.* John 1:1-18; 1 John 1:1-4; Luke 1:1-4; and 2 Pet. 1:16-21).

The Predominant Characteristics of Special Revelation

When we examine what the Bible, as a whole, says about the predominant characteristics of this special revelation, we discover that 1) it is progressive in nature; 2) that in Jesus Christ, the progressive revelation of God's plan to redeem and reconcile both humanity and creation is given its fullest, most complete and final form, which 3) is then permanently recorded and given its permanent definition in the New Testament writings. Indeed, this progressive, Christ-centered, special revelation of God and the divine redemptive plan is best summed up by the author of the Book of Hebrews:

> Long ago God spoke many times and in many ways to our ancestors through the prophets. But now in these final days, he has spoken to us through his Son. God promised everything to the Son as an inheritance, and through the Son he made the universe and everything in it. The Son reflects God's own glory, and everything about him represents God exactly. He sustains the universe by the mighty power of his command. After he died to cleanse us from the stain of sin, he sat down in the place of honor at the right hand of the majestic God of heaven. So we must listen very carefully to the truth we have heard, or we may drift from it. The message God delivered through angels has always proved true, and the [Israelites] were punished for every violation of [the Mosaic] law and for every act of disobedience. What makes us think that we can escape if we are indifferent to the great salvation announced by the Lord Jesus himself? [his gospel] was passed on to us by [the Apostles] who heard him speak, and God verified [their] message by signs and wonders and various miraculous gifts of the Holy Spirit whenever he chose to do so (Heb. 1:1-3; 2:1-4, NLT).

Moreover, not only were the apostles themselves convinced that Jesus' ministry and message were the fulfillment of the prophetic revelation given through Moses and the Prophets regarding the coming of Messiah and his message for all the nations (*cf.* Deut. 18:18-19 and Isa. 42:1-7 with Matt. 12:9-21, John 6:10-15, and Acts 10:14-48), but their own eyewitness account and interpretation of Jesus' life, message, death, and resurrection,(as recorded in the New Testament writings) further confirmed the truth and relevance of God's revelation in Christ, promised in Moses and the Prophets. As Peter says:

> For we did not follow cleverly devised stories when we told you about the coming of our Lord Jesus in power, but we were eyewitnesses of his majesty. He received honor and glory from God the Father when the voice came to him from the Majestic Glory, saying, "This is my Son, whom I love; with him I am well pleased." We ourselves heard this voice that came from heaven when we were with him on the sacred mountain. Therefore, we have further confirmation that the Old Testament prophetic message is completely reliable, and you will do well to pay attention to it, as to a light shining in a dark place, until the Day dawns and the Morning Star rises in your hearts. Above all else, though, you must understand that no Scriptural prophecy came from the prophets' self-generated speculations. Rather, the prophets, though human, spoke from God as they were carried along by the Holy Spirit (2 Pet. 1:16-21, my rendering).

Historical Views of General and Special Revelation

But let us get back to the relationship between general and special revelation. What, if anything, can we make of the knowledge of God that is gained from the light of nature and the works of creation? And what is the relationship of this natural knowledge of God to the knowledge given us through special revelation of Scripture? To the first question, there have been three basic answers given in the West by philosophers and theologians. We briefly state and comment on them as follows:

1. ***The Deistic View.*** This was the predominant view among European philosophers in the eighteenth century. According to this view, what we know about God through rational and empirical observation of the natural world and ourselves is the most certain knowledge we can ever have. Any supposed "special revelation" of God must be measured, judged, and corrected by this rational and empirical knowledge. Furthermore, it cannot contradict the "natural theology" we have already discovered through our

rational, scientific study of the natural world and of ourselves. So if the Bible, as "special revelation," appears to teach anything contrary to our "natural theology," it is the Bible that must be reinterpreted or rejected. But no orthodox Christian, who takes the teaching of the Bible seriously, can rationally or ethically embrace this viewpoint and live by it. As Dr. Shirley Guthrie comments:

> For instance, if I think I have learned what is possible and impossible according to the God-given physical laws of the natural world and I read in the Bible about a God who breaks those laws and does the impossible, I must automatically conclude the Bible is wrong in what it says, or explain it in such a way that it only seems to speak of a God who acts in an unnatural way. Could God break God's own law—the law we find operating in the world God made? If I decide that according to the laws of nature that the biblical claim that God loves God's enemies and commands us to do the same is unnatural, then I must refuse to obey those commands. The mainstream of Christian thought has, of course, rejected this extreme position that special revelation is to be judged by and made to conform to "natural religion." It is obviously a subtle way of our deciding what God can and must be and do...There is no place for a real revelation at all. Revelation means that something *new* is made known. But this extreme position will hear and accept only what we already know or think we know or can learn by ourselves.[2]

2. *The Complementarian View*. A second, more moderate view is that while natural revelation cannot dictate what the form and content of special revelation can and must take, it can give us an incomplete, preliminary, or preparatory knowledge of God. It can at least show us that there is a supreme being, and give a hint as to this being's power, wisdom, and goodness. But it is not sufficient to bring us to a knowledge that this God, besides being a creator, is also a judge and redeemer. Due to human finiteness and fallenness, the knowledge of God derived from natural theology or general revelation, is at best incomplete, and so must be supplemented and corrected by the knowledge of God which can only come through special revelation, such as that given through prophets, Christ, and the Bible. Moreover, through a judicious appeal to natural evidences, we are able to show how general revelation and special revelation complement and support each other, enabling people to recognize the full and complete revelation God has given in Jesus Christ, and through the Bible that both permanently records and interprets this special revelation. And it is this second view which has, historically, been held by both Catholic and Protestant philosophers and theologians over the centuries, and remains the majority view of most orthodox Christians.

3. *The Adversarial View*. This view denies any validity to a natural theology. According to this view, while it is true we might have an ambiguous "sense" of God's existence through observation and analysis of the natural world and ourselves, we can have no true, certain knowledge of God. For when we begin to say something about God based on the knowledge derived from observing nature and ourselves, we're only talking about our own ideas and feelings, not about the God who is "absolutely other." There is no "natural theology" that conveys any true, certain knowledge of God. The only way we can truly know God is for God to be revealed to us through the proclamation of Jesus Christ; which proclamation constitutes "The Word of God." This view is primarily identified with Karl Barth and his followers.

But in light of what is said in Psalm 19; Acts 14:14-18; and Romans 1:18-2:16, this seems to be another extreme view of general and special revelation that is not helpful in proclaiming, defending, and confirming the Christian Faith. As for myself, I hold to a form of the second view. While God provided a true revelation of the divine being and character in creation, it was limited by human finiteness and fallenness. Therefore, it was necessary for God to provide a special revelation that would truly interpret, supplement, and correct the true, but limited knowledge we gain on the basis of general revelation. And in the next chapter, I will discuss why it was necessary for this special revelation to be preserved in permanent written form, so as to prevent either its later loss or corruption.

End Notes

1. Gerald L. Schroeder, *The Science of God: The Convergence of Scientific and Biblical Wisdom*, p. 21.

2. Shirley Guthrie, *Christian Doctrine, Revised Edition*, pp. 43-44.

The Necessity of a Written Revelation

Francis Turretin, (or Francesco Turrettini, the original Italian name), a French Protestant theologian of the seventeenth century, explained that just as parents use different methods of education and training through the different stages of their development, so God has used different methods of education and training in the different stages of his people's development throughout redemptive history:

> For, just as in the economy of the natural order parents change the manner of dealing with their children as they grow older, so that infants are first directed by the spoken word, then by the voice of a teacher and the reading of books, and are finally freed from the guidance of the teacher and learn on their own from books, so the Heavenly Father, who instructs his people as the head of a family (Deut. 8:5), taught the church, when it was still young and childish, by the spoken word, the most simple form of revelation. Then, as it began to mature and was established under the Law in its early youth, he taught it both by the spoken word, because of continuing childishness, and by writing, because of the beginnings of maturity, under the Apostles' time. But when the Church had reached adulthood, under the Gospel, God wanted his people to be satisfied with the most perfect form of revelation, Scripture.[1]

Now, while some Christians of a charismatic persuasion would disagree with Turretin, saying that God still speaks to us by both a book (Scripture) and by the spoken word (the gift of prophecy), I think most would still agree that God does train and discipline his children, in various ways, in accordance with the times and circumstances of their lives. And difficult and dangerous circumstances call for appropriate measures of guidance and instruction. So what we want to focus on in our present discussion is why it was necessary for God's revealed word through Christ and his Apostles to be written down.

The Nature, Scope and Limitations of Oral Tradition

Craig Blomberg, in his book *The Historical Reliability of the Synoptic Gospels*, surveys various studies of the practices first century Jewish rabbis and Greco-Roman philosophers used in teaching their pupils to vividly remember and pass on their teaching to others. These studies found that in both the Jewish and Greco-Roman culture of that day, pupils took shorthand notes and learned rigorous rules of memorization in order to accurately recall the key acts and teachings of their rabbi or philosopher teacher.

While they could paraphrase the teaching to some degree, or topically arrange the events of the rabbi's life or portions of his teaching, religious-social conventions of the day frowned upon the pupils fabricating any stories or teachings not originating with the rabbi or philosopher and which could be exposed and refuted as false by those who had actually seen and heard the rabbi or philosopher themselves. And this memorized story of the rabbi and his teaching was known as *oral tradition*. As long as people were willing to abide by the rules of oral tradition, there was no problem. And in many cases, the difference between contemporary oral and written tradition (*i.e.*, shorthand notes) was mainly that of emphasis, not substance, of teaching.

Of course, certain liberal form critics have argued that the "oral" Jesus traditions, as later adapted and incorporated by the New Testament writers in general, and by the gospel writers in particular, were greatly corrupted and/or embellished. However, Dr. Blomberg shows why this charge is without any solid warrant:

> Several considerations challenge the notion that the stories of what Jesus did and said would have been significantly distorted as they

were passed on by word of mouth. (1) The short period of time between actual events described (c. A.D. 27-30) and the time in which Mark wrote his Gospel (c. A.D. 70-75 at the latest, and probably pre-70) distinguishes the formation of the gospels from other allegedly parallel processes of oral transmission in antiquity, which generally span several centuries. Eyewitnesses of Jesus' ministry, including hostile ones, could easily have refuted and discredited the Christian claims during this period if they were in any way mistaken. (2) The relatively short span of time was probably even shorter than the forty year maximum just noted, since Q (see pp. 12-13) probably dates from the 50's. Additionally, as with the disciples of the ancient Jewish rabbis, Jesus' followers may well have kept privately written notes while passing on the tradition orally in public. There is no reason why Jesus' disciples could not have begun such note-taking even while he was still alive, since Jesus sent them out on their own at least on two missions to preach the gospel. After the ascension this practice would have become even more likely. (3) The so-called rules of transmission of the tradition are anything but "laws". E. P. Sanders, in one of the earliest studies to use computer technology to gather data relevant to biblical studies, analyzed in detail the gospel traditions which have been preserved in textual variants, the early church fathers and New Testament apocrypha, and demonstrated that no consistent trends exist concerning the lengthening or shortening, preservation or distortion of the tradition. If anything, other shorter studies have demonstrated a slight tendency for detailed material to become abbreviated, condensed, more stereotyped and less vivid as the stories of Jesus were continually retold in the Gentile world, all precisely the opposite of what the first form critics alleged! Certainly this trend is observable if one compares parallel passages in Mark and Luke, and to a lesser extent in Mark and Matthew.[2]

Now, when one studies Acts and the letters of Peter and Paul in the New Testament, it becomes clear that the content of the apostles' oral and written teaching is substantially the same though, depending on the nature of the audience being addressed, there is a difference in emphasis.

However, long before they were dead and cold in their graves, the apostles were faced with false teachers who, wanting to "modernize" the gospel and build their own group of followers, began distorting and corrupting the "oral" Christian traditions quite early. Some heretics were even bold enough to forge letters in Peter and Paul's names that taught things contrary to "the sound doctrine" the apostles had taught in the churches they and their associates had founded.

Paul, for example, when he heard how false teachers were distorting his teaching about the second coming of Christ, dispatched a letter to the Thessalonian churches, refuting the heretics and reminding his converts of what he had actually taught them:

> "Concerning the coming of our Lord Jesus Christ and our being gathered to him, we ask you, brothers and sisters, not to become easily unsettled or alarmed by the teaching allegedly from us — whether by a prophecy or by word of mouth or by letter — asserting that the Day of the Lord has already come. Don't let anyone deceive you in any way, for that Day will not come until the rebellion occurs and the man of lawlessness is revealed, the man doomed to destruction. Don't you remember that when I was with you I used to tell you these things?...So then, brothers and sisters, stand firm and hold fast to the teachings we passed on to you, whether by word of mouth or by letter" (2 Thess. 2:1-15, TNIV).

Peter, while in Rome and sensing that terrible persecution by Nero was drawing near, also saw the rising danger of false teachers, who were perverting the gospel message. So he wrote two letters to Christians under his care, reminding them of what he had actually taught them about the life, words, and deeds of the Lord Jesus Christ. And in the second of these letters, he told the readers that the purpose of both letters had not only been to stimulate them to wholesome thinking and godly living, but also to warn them against heretical false teachers, providing them with a permanent reminder of the gospel he had preached to them.

> "I think it is only right, while I yet live in this body, to refresh your

memory...because I know I will soon depart my earthly tent, just as our Lord Jesus Christ made clear to me. And I will make every effort to see that, after my departure, you will have a lasting means to keep remembering these things I taught you" (2 Pet. 1:12-13, my translation).

Though there is some debate as to which document he was referring to as his written legacy, many Christian scholars, from Irenaeus to B. B. Warfield, have argued he was referring to the Gospel of Mark, which his disciple and missionary associate, John Mark, wrote down as a record and summary of Peter's teaching and preaching.

Then, in addition to the problems posed by heretical distortions of the gospel mentioned above, there was the need for historically reliable, well-written documentation of Jesus' life and teachings that could serve to both establish new converts in their faith, as well as to provide authoritative answers to the questions and objections regarding Christianity their non-Christian friends would be sure to raise. J. G. Dunn, concerning this very issue, states:

> In terms of human nature as we know it today, it would have been very unusual if the followers of such a leader had not been concerned to preserve memories of the exploits and utterances that drew them to him and sustained their loyalty to him. There are two factors operative in the case of Jesus that would go a long way towards quickening the element of "human interest" in Jesus: The first is the degree to which Jesus himself featured as part of the earliest Christian proclamation. Jesus was not remembered merely as one who had provided a system of teaching or a philosophy or a spirituality, which could be preserved and practiced without reference to the original teacher. It is true that the focus of the evangelistic preaching centered very strongly on the end events of his life on earth (*i.e.*, his death and resurrection). Nevertheless, it would be surprising indeed if the disciples had not looked to Jesus' own earlier ministry and pattern of teaching and life-style to provide some kind of guidelines for their own life of faith. The second is the fact that Christianity from the beginning was an evangelistic faith. It did not withdraw into the desert as a closed sect where all the

members would know the facts of its founding, and so there would be no need to record them. From the first, it sought to gain converts, and very soon converts from further afield than Palestine, including Gentiles. Human curiosity being what it is, most of these converts would certainly have wanted to hear more about the Jesus in whom they had believed. It would be odd indeed to imagine Christian congregations meeting throughout the eastern Mediterranean, who in their regular gatherings were concerned with only the study of the Jewish scriptures, the message of Jesus' death and resurrection, and with waiting for the return of their risen Lord--and who were quite unconcerned to recall and reflect on the ministry and teaching of Jesus while on earth. On the contrary, it was precisely these memories, these traditions, which they were most likely to want to share and celebrate together — the founding traditions which gave them their distinctive identity.[3]

Indeed, Luke, the missionary companion of the apostle Paul, in his two volume history of Jesus and the earliest Christians, which we know as *The Gospel of Luke* and *The Acts of the Apostles*, states that this was one of the main purposes in his writing this two volume history:

> Most honorable Theophilus: Many people have written accounts about the events that took place among us. They used as their source material the reports circulating among us from the early disciples and other eyewitnesses of what God has done in fulfillment of his promises. Having carefully investigated all these accounts from the beginning, I have decided to write a careful summary for you, to reassure you of the truth of all that you were taught (Luke 1:1-4, NLT).

Luke was not the first to attempt to write a history of Jesus' life and ministry. Others had done so before him. Therefore, he recognizes and acknowledges the value of these earlier works, as well as noting his use of these sources in producing his own historical record and interpretation of Jesus' life. But he wants to assure Theophilus that what he has written is historically reliable and true, confirming the absolute truth of the gospel Theophilus has received and believed. And we know from both the extant internal and external evidence available to us, this two volume history was written AD 58-62, during the time of Paul's first imprisonment in Rome. Paul himself not only had a high regard for the truthfulness and reliability of Luke's writing, but in 1 Timothy 5:17-18, when quoting Scripture as the basis for his instructions regarding both honoring and supporting faithful elders, he appeals to both Deuteronomy 25:4 and Luke 10:7. So Paul regarded Luke's writings as not only historically reliable documents, but also as the inspired and authoritative word of God! Furthermore, over the last 170 years, archaeological discoveries in Europe and the Middle East have abundantly proven that not only was Luke a good theologian, but also among the most reliable of first century historians. Not surprisingly, his two volume history continues, even in our own time, to have great value in proclaiming, defending, and confirming the truth of the gospel to converts and skeptics alike.

So for all the above reasons, we see why it was necessary that the revelation of God's redemptive words and deeds, especially as revealed in and through the Lord Jesus Christ, had to be written down and preserved in a permanent and reliable textual form. In the next chapter, we will further explore the connection between the gospel writers' dual role as reliable historians and theologians.

End Notes

1. Francis Turrettini, *The Doctrine of Scripture*, pp. 28-29.

2. Craig Blomberg, "New Methods in Gospel Study," *The Historical Reliability of the Gospels*, pp. 24-25.

3. J.G. Dunn, "The Historicity of the Synoptic Gospels," *Crisis in Christology*, pp. 201-202.

The New Testament and Ancient Greco-Roman Historians

As incredible as it may seem, there are still some people who believe that Jesus of Nazareth never existed. They are impressed with the arguments of certain atheistic philosophers that Jesus was merely a legendary religious figure, or mythical hero, conjured up by the creative imagination of a band of disenchanted first century Jews. "But, in fact, a man such as Jesus of Nazareth, as the early church regarded him," argue these historical skeptics, "never actually existed. His story, as recounted in the New Testament, is nothing but religious myth and legend."

However, many modern historians and biblical scholars, who are by no means religious fundamentalists, judge this atheistic claim as being fallacious. Using long-established criteria of historical investigation and verification[1], they would argue that various early Jewish and Greco-Roman sources, having no direct contact with the New Testament itself, bear a reliable independent testimony that: Jesus of Nazareth, a Jewish rabbi, had actually existed; that he had been regarded and condemned, by the official Judaism of his day, to be a Messianic pretender and sorcerer; that under Pontus Pilate, the Procurator of Judea, he had been crucified as a criminal; that his followers, who became known as "Christians," confessed him as Lord and God; and that they had spread their religion throughout the Roman Empire well before AD 100.

So what can we learn from these non-Christian witnesses about Jesus and the earliest Christians? And how much does it jibe with the story of Jesus and his apostles as we find it in the New Testament? Though we could have consulted several ancient Jewish and Greco-Roman sources, we will consider three who give us the fullest account of Jesus and the religious movement he founded. Then we will consider a couple of the New Testament writers themselves.

Three Ancient Witnesses to Jesus and the Early Christians

Our first witness is rabbi Eliezer (c. AD 70-100). He was a Pharisaic scribe and teacher who lived and ministered in Palestine during the post-AD 70 period, which means he would have known about Jesus, the Jerusalem church, and the beginnings of the Jewish-Roman War (AD 66-70). In his commentary on Numbers 23:19, which was preserved in the later Palestinian Mishnah and Talmud, he made the following critique of Jesus of Nazareth and his followers:

> "Balaam looked forth and saw that there was a man, born of a woman, who would rise up and seek to make himself God, and cause the whole world to go astray. Therefore, God gave power to the voice of Balaam that all the peoples of the world might hear, and thus he spoke, 'Give heed that ye go not astray after that man: for it is written, 'God is not a man that he should lie.' And if this man says he is God, he is a liar, and he will deceive and say he departeth and cometh again at the end. He saith and shall not perform."[2]

Although he does not mention Jesus of Nazareth by name, rabbi Eliezer's reference to "a man, born of a woman," was (as this rabbi well-knew) a designation given to Jesus by the earliest Christians, indicating that his virgin birth, death on the cross, and resurrection from the dead were the fulfillment of both Genesis 3:15 and Isaiah 7:14, which were regarded as messianic prophecies regarding both Messiah's person and redemptive work (*cf.* Matt. 1:18-25 and Gal. 4:4). And Eliezer's statement regarding Jesus that "[he] departeth and cometh again at the end" also reveals he rejected and opposed Jesus and his followers. For he apparently was aware of the common Christian teaching that Jesus of Nazareth, as the risen and exalted Messiah, would come at the end of the age to judge both the living and the dead (*cf.* Acts 3:11-24; Rom. 2:12-15; and 2 Thess. 1:6-10). So there can be no doubt as to the polemic nature of rabbi Eliezer's commentary.

Nevertheless, this testimony of a leading Pharisaic leader, who certainly was not favorably inclined towards the "Nazarene sect" and its founder, reveals four historical facts about Jesus and the earliest Christians:

- Jesus of Nazareth actually existed, and he was the founder of a religious movement that began as a sect of Judaism
- Jesus' life, words and miraculous deeds were of such a nature that his followers were compelled to both acknowledge him as God in the flesh, who would return at the end of the age to judge all humanity (*cf.* Matt. 1:20-23 and Acts 10:34-43)
- Pharisaic Judaism, as represented by rabbi Eliezer himself, regarded Jesus of Nazareth as a false prophet, a messianic pretender, and a sorcerer. Not only do numerous New Testament texts confirm this, but so do the writings of the Early Church Fathers, such as Justin Martyr's *Against Trypho and the Jews*
- Christians were definitely proclaiming Jesus as God and Savior throughout the Roman Empire, making converts among both Jews and Gentiles (*cf.* Acts 26:1-29 and 28:17-31).

Our second witness is Cornelius Tacitus (c. AD 55-120). He was a Roman senator who began his career under Emperor Vespasian (reigned AD 69-79), entered the imperial consulship under Emperor Nerva in AD 97 and served as Proconsul of Asia from AD 112-113 under Emperor Trajan. Tacitus was a very capable orator and writer, having the reputation of being a careful and reliable historian of the empire. However, he was very critical of certain earlier emperors and their policies which, in his opinion, had undermined the moral and social well-being of the Roman people. And he often emphasized the noble contributions and achievements of the Roman aristocracy, which he saw as the true basis of Rome's greatness.

Tacitus wrote five historical works.[3] In two of them, the *Annals of Imperial Rome* and *The Histories of Imperial Rome*, Tacitus makes passing references to Jesus of Nazareth and the earliest Christians.

Since he was a Roman aristocrat and politician, Tacitus, like most of the Roman nobility, venerated the illustrious past of Rome's culture and institutions. But he disliked anything that brought change in Roman society and culture, especially foreign superstitions like Christianity. But having been proconsul of Asia, where a large segment of the population was Christians, Tacitus knew this new religious movement could not be ignored. Therefore, he grudgingly gave this religious "superstition" what he considered "appropriate" recognition. And so in chapter fifteen of his *Annals of Imperial Rome*, where he condemns Emperor Nero for the burning of Rome, he makes a brief reference to Jesus and the early Christians:

> But all human efforts, all the lavish gifts of the emperor, and all the propitiations of the gods, did not banish the sinister belief that the conflagration was the result of an [imperial] order. Consequently, to get rid of the report, Nero fastened the guilt and inflicted the most exquisite tortures on a class of people hated for their abominations, called Christians by the populace. *Christus*, from whom the name had its origin, suffered the extreme penalty during the reign of Tiberius at the hands of one of our procurators, Pontus Pilate, and a deadly superstition, thus checked for the moment, broke out in Judaea, the first source of evil, but also in Rome, where all things hideous and shameful from every part of the world meet and become popular. Accordingly, an arrest was first made of all who confessed; then, upon information, an immense multitude was convicted, not so much of the crime of arson, as of hatred of the human race (*Annals*, 15:44, 2-5).[4]

And it is in the second paragraph of this commentary on Nero's reign that Tacitus confirms the historicity of the "Jesus tradition" that not only formed the core of the apostles' own preaching and teaching, but which was also incorporated in and preserved in the New Testament Gospels and Epistles:

- The public career of Jesus of Nazareth, whom the early Christians had proclaimed as Christ or Messiah, occurred during the reign of Emperor Tiberius (*cf.* Luke 3:1)
- Pontus Pilate was the Roman procurator or governor of Judea when Christ was arrested and crucified (*cf.* Matt. 27:2; Lk. 3:1 and 23:1-5; John 18:28-30; Acts 3:13 and 13:28)
- Christ was executed as a criminal, suffering "the extreme

penalty" — that of crucifixion, the form of execution ordered by Pilate at the request of the Jewish leaders (*cf.* Matt. 27:24-26; Mk. 15:1-15; Lk. 23:2, 20-25; John 19:4-16)

- This religious movement, which had begun as a Jewish sect in Judea, and which proclaimed Jesus of Nazareth as both Messiah and Lord, had spread to Rome well before AD 64 Furthermore, the Christians refusal to acknowledge anyone else but Jesus as Lord was considered an act of treason, a crime against the human race who acknowledged Caesar as Lord. This was the real reason, as Tacitus admits, why the Christians had been and continued to be persecuted and killed.

Our third and last witness is Flavius Josephus (c. AD 37-100). Josephus was born in Jerusalem, grew up as a member of a priestly family, and then was further trained by the Pharisees. His career as politician and governor of Galilee began during the reign of Emperor Nero. During the early stages of the Jewish-Roman War (AD 66-73), he became a resistance leader and fought against the Roman army. When he and his troops were defeated by the Romans at Jotapata (c. AD 67), Josephus realized the futility of the Jewish resistance to Rome, and so joined the Roman forces as an interpreter and mediator between the Jews and Romans. However, most of his Jewish countrymen considered him a turncoat and traitor, and so Josephus' attempts at mediating a peace settlement failed. Consequently, the Jewish rebellion was essentially crushed in AD 70, though the garrison at Masada wasn't taken until three years later. The Romans destroyed Jerusalem and the temple, with vast numbers of Palestinian Jews either being executed or deported as slaves by the victorious Roman legions.

After the war, Josephus went to Rome where, for services rendered, he was made a Roman citizen and a courtier of Emperor Vespasian. During his years in Rome, he wrote two of his best known historical works: *History of the Jewish War*, which even now is a highly valued account of this tragic conflict, and *The Antiquities of the Jews*, a history of the Jewish people from the creation of the world until the Jewish-Roman War. As would be expected, Josephus casts the character and achievements of the Jewish people in the most favorable light he can, without offending his Roman benefactors. And those whom he considered personal enemies or enemies of the imperial court, he treats in a pejorative manner. Nevertheless, Josephus is still a generally reliable and informative history, according to G. A. Williamson, an English professor of Greco-Roman history:

> Of course, Josephus was not a critical historian; he swallowed openmouthed the statements of his informants...His passion for hyperbole enables him to write of rivers of blood that extinguished the fires of Jerusalem and so on...All the people he disliked were scoundrels, bandits, terrorists, tyrants, agitators, and the like...As for Titus, the flattery poured upon him by Josephus is distasteful in the extreme.... But when all this has been admitted, the fact remains that while, as all scholars agree, we must use the greatest caution in accepting at its face value any statement Josephus makes about himself or his personal enemies, when he has no axe to grind and is not engaging in patent exaggeration, he is an informative and reliable historian.[5]

Now that we know something about both Josephus and his strengths and weaknesses as a historian, we can better evaluate his statements about Jesus of Nazareth and the earliest Christians. In a passage known as the *Testimonium Flavianum*, found in his *Antiquities of the Jews*, Josephus (even though an unbelieving Pharisee) gives some illuminating testimony about Jesus and his followers. According to the textual criticism of the best historians, the testimony reads as follows:

> About this time there lived Jesus, a wise man. For he was one who wrought surprising feats and was a teacher of such people as accept the truth gladly. He won over many Jews and many of the Greeks. He was the [so-called] Messiah. When Pilate, upon hearing him accused by the men of highest standing among us, had condemned him to be crucified, those who had in the first place come to love him did not give up their affection for him. For on the third day, [so they claimed,] he appeared to them, restored to life. And the tribe of Christians [so called after him], to this day has still not disappeared.

Not only was Jesus of Nazareth a historical figure, but, according to

Josephus there were certain facts about him and his followers that were generally known to be true as well:

- Jesus had been a "wise man...and...teacher" who had had an extensive ministry in Judea, which included the performance of "surprising feats" or miracles (*cf.* Mk. 6:1-6; Lk. 4:14-22; Acts 2:22; 10:38)
- Allegations made by the Jewish leaders in Jerusalem were, in part, responsible for Jesus' arrest, conviction, and execution as a criminal and enemy of Rome (*cf.* Matt. 27:12-14; Mk. 15:1-5; Lk. 23:1-25)
- Pontus Pilate, the Roman governor, for whatever personal reasons, had concurred with the Jewish leaders' charges against Jesus, and so had authorized his execution (*cf.* Matt. 27:15-26; Mk. 15:6-15; Lk. 23:13-25)
- A large number of Jews and Greeks had become Jesus' followers after gladly hearing and accepting his message, whether they had heard it directly from him or from his followers, who regarded him as Messiah (*cf.* Acts 2:22-41; 3:1-4; 11:19-26). And the "tribe of Christians," at the time Josephus was writing *The Antiquities of the Jews* (c. AD 90), remained a strong, vigorous religious movement which, out of undying love for its martyred founder, continued spreading that Jesus was Messiah and Lord.

Conclusions to be Drawn from These Non-Christian Sources

Now, if Jesus of Nazareth had never existed, nor had said or done anything that would have led his disciples to believe that he was both Messiah and Son of God, not only would the New Testament itself never have been written, but neither would these Jewish and Greco-Roman writers have found it necessary to discuss and debunk Christianity. W. D. Davies sums up this matter well:

> The passages referred to above, both Jewish and Gentile, sufficiently attest the historicity of Jesus. That Jesus was a crucified teacher who caused embarrassment to Judaism and to Rome is clear. For our present purposes this evidence is adequate; it does pin down the existence of

Jesus of Nazareth beyond doubt. And it is easy to understand why Jewish and Gentile sources do not reveal more. Today, Christianity is a worldwide religion, and Jesus has become the object of reverence for millions. In the first century, the Christian movement and its Lord were insignificant and, for Roman writers especially, objects of suspicion and contempt. The silence of the non-Christian sources, except for the details given above, is understandable. Beyond the bare fact of Jesus as a crucified teacher, it is from the specifically Christian sources that knowledge about him and his church must be learned. This is another way of claiming what was asserted at the end of [our] last chapter, that Jesus, as a figure of history, gains significance only through those who responded to him.[6]

So if we want to know the true story on Jesus and the religious movement he founded, we must turn, as Davies has reminded us, to the New Testament writings. For only there will we find the full testimony of those who encountered and had to explain to themselves and others this most unique historical person.

End Notes

1. See, for example, Craig Blomberg, *The Historical Reliability of the Gospels;* Luke Timothy Johnson, *The Real Jesus*; John P. Maier, *Jesus: A Marginalized Jew*; Lee Strobel, *The Case for the Real Jesus*; and N. T. Wright, *Jesus and the Victory of God*.

2. Paul Barnett, "Did Jesus Exist? Early Non-Christian References," *Is the New Testament History?*, pp.16-31

3. Dialogue on Oratory, which discusses the decline of oratory in Rome after Cicero; The Origins of the German Tribes, which is recognized as the major source about the German tribes before their invasions of Rome; The Life of Gnaeus Julius Agricola, a historical biography of a Roman senator and general who was instrumental in the conquest of Britain; The Annals of Imperial Rome, a history of Julio-Claudian Rome from AD 14-68; and The Histories of Imperial Rome, a history of Flavian Rome from AD 69-96

4. Barnett, "Did Jesus Exist? Early Non-Christian References," p. 20-22.

5. G. A. Williamson," Introduction," *Josephus: The Jewish War: An English Translation,* Penguin Classics, pp. 14-15.

6. W. D. Davies," The Historicity of Jesus," *Invitation to the New Testament: A Guide to the Main Witnesses,* p. 71.

The New Testament Writers as Historians and Theologians

In the previous chapter, we considered the non-Christian witnesses to Jesus and the Earliest Christians. We found that while they were valuable in confirming both the historicity of Jesus and the religious movement he founded, we also found that this testimony was very limited and often hostile. Only in the New Testament, as Davies pointed out, can we find the full record of the Christians' own understanding of Jesus and how he had impacted them and their world. In this chapter we will deal with the charge that because of their religious commitments as Christian preachers and apologists, they were not able to engage in careful research and critical thinking as historians.

Reasons Why the New Testament Writers Could Not "Fabricate" Jesus Stories

Contrary to charges that some have made, it is not true that the New Testament writers were free to misrepresent what was actually known about Jesus and the earliest Christians, nor to fabricate events and sayings attributed to Jesus and the apostles that were widely known as never having occurred or having been said. First of all, the genuine historicity of the gospel story was crucial to the success of the early Christian church's task of evangelism and apologetics. For if it had failed to faithfully and accurately confirm what the historical Jesus had actually said and done, then its evangelists and apologists would never had succeeded in winning converts to Christ. For who would seriously consider responding to their message that Jesus was the Messiah, promised by the Old Testament prophets, and not be curious as to the historical facts that validated their message?

In order to answer questions that would inevitably arise regarding Jesus' true identity, the content of his teaching, as well as regarding the purpose of his life, death, and resurrection, it was necessary that those engaged in the task of evangelizing and discipling new converts know enough of "the true story of Jesus" to answer those very questions. For if they could not have given reliable and verifiable answers to these questions about who Jesus was, what he actually said and did, and what the true meaning and significance of it all was, then nobody would have paid any serious attention to them. Let us be very clear about this: If the early Christian preachers and teachers could not give honest answers to honest questions about Jesus, then the Christian movement would have been still-born from the beginning. New converts not only wanted to know what Jesus had said and done, they also wanted a pattern of lifestyle and worship endorsed by the founder of their religious movement, as was noted by J.G. Dunn in the previous chapter:

> In terms of human nature as we know it today, it would have been very unusual if the followers of such a leader had not been concerned to preserve memories of the exploits and utterances that drew them to him and sustained their loyalty to him. There are two factors operative in the case of Jesus that would go a long way towards quickening the element of "human interest" in Jesus: The first is the degree to which Jesus himself featured as part of the earliest Christian proclamation. Jesus was not remembered merely as one who had provided a system of teaching or a philosophy or a spirituality, which could be preserved and practiced without reference to the original teacher. It is true that the focus of the evangelistic preaching centered very strongly on the end events of his life on earth (*i.e.*, his death and resurrection). Nevertheless, it would be surprising indeed if the disciples had not looked to Jesus' own earlier ministry and pattern of teaching and life-style to provide some kind of guidelines for their own life of faith.[1]

And, as we have noted elsewhere, the notion that the Jesus tradition(s) utilized by the New Testament writers had been primarily oral in nature and so subject to a great deal of alteration and distortion before they were written down has been disproved by the evidence gathered together from modern studies of oral and written traditions conducted over the last thirty years. From these more recent critical studies, many New Testament scholars have concluded that the time between the circulation of the oral and written Jesus traditions and the writing and distribution of Mark's Gospel (ca. AD 50-55), regarded as the earliest of such writing, was less than 30 years—far too short a time for any substantial revision or alteration of the Jesus traditions to have occurred. Furthermore, since he is supposed to have produced this first written account of Jesus' life and ministry at a time when both Peter and Paul were still alive and who "knew the true story," they could have denounced Mark's account as fraudulent if it had radically altered or departed from historical reality. And then there is also the matter of the socio-religious resistance to "revisionist" histories that existed in first century Israel, and even among contemporary Greco-Roman philosophers and historians.

Ancient peoples, much like people today, did not greatly appreciate "revisionist" histories that so radically altered their cherished historical, national, or religious identity and mission to such a degree that it was rendered false and invalid. Therefore, the modern notion that the Jesus tradition became very corrupt and embellished, stumbles over three well-known facts regarding the preservation and transmission of religious or philosophical traditions in the ancient Jewish and Greco-Roman societies. Two we have already briefly considered: 1) The need for a reliable record and interpretation of Jesus' life, words and deeds so that early Christian evangelists and apologists could address the questions and challenges that would arise concerning the historicity of Christianity; and 2) the extremely short time existing between the circulation of the early oral and written Jesus traditions, and the writing of the Four Gospels, of which both Mark (c. AD-55) and Luke (c. AD 58-62) were written not more than 30 years later. And then there is the third fact of the socio-religious "quality controls" that prevented the New Testament writers from fabricating Jesus stories and sayings.

On the nature of these controls and their constraint on the New Testament writers' supposed creative inventiveness, John R. Edwards comments,

Suffice it to say that there are a number of "quality controls" in the New Testament to argue against such fanciful inventiveness. The Gospel writers did not wildly invent material about Jesus, but they were quite careful with the Jesus tradition. This is shown by the following:

- Many eyewitnesses of Jesus were still alive when the Gospels were written. These witnesses functioned as gatekeepers and custodians of "the faith that was once for all entrusted to the saints" (Jude 3). The wild inventiveness supposed by the radical critics is not found in the New Testament, but rather in certain second-century documents (*e.g.*, the Infancy Narratives of Jesus, the Protoevangelium of James) that were produced later where Jesus traditions circulated in communities separated from the Apostolic church.
- The rabbinic method of teaching by rote favored accurate and careful transmission of Jesus traditions as opposed to novel interpretations.
- The presence of embarrassing and even problematic material in the Gospels (*e.g.*, Mark 9:1; 14:71) speaks against the inventiveness of the early church, even when the church might have profited from it.
- A comparison of the Epistles with the Gospels reveals that neither Paul's words nor those of other New Testament writers have been projected back onto the mouth of Jesus. No passage from Paul (or any other of the New Testament letters) can be found in the Gospels or on the lips of Jesus. No Pauline concept, such as the "body of Christ," "righteousness by faith," "under the law," or "flesh" is attributed to Jesus...If the early church were avidly and indiscriminately putting words into the mouth of Jesus, we should expect to find at least some of the material from the Epistles in the Gospels or on the lips of Jesus. Since we do not, we ought to conclude that the gospel material is not extrapolated from the early church and then projected onto Jesus.
- Finally, the supposed inventiveness of the early church meets a final stumbling block in the Gentile question. According to Acts

and the Epistles, the preaching of the gospel to the Gentiles and their admission into the church was the burning question of the early church. This issue, however, is virtually absent from the Gospels. Had the church actively engaged framing "Jesus material" according to its needs and interests, surely it would have developed sayings on the Gentile question. The fact that such sayings are virtually absent from the Gospels [strongly] argues in favor of the historical reliability of the material that is there.[2]

A Further Consideration of Luke as Both Historian and Theologian

One would think that the above evidences and arguments would be more than sufficient to dismiss the false charges laid against the New Testament writers' reliability and credibility as historical chroniclers and interpreters of Jesus life and ministry. And then there are clear statements by the New Testament authors, such as Luke, that what we are being offered is a true and reliable account. In the "Introduction" to his two volume history (Luke 1:1-4), Luke tells Theophilus that after careful investigation of the facts, he wrote this record of Jesus and his followers so as to reassure him of the truth of what he had been taught about the rise and spread of Christianity. Concerning this introduction or preface of Luke's, Darrell L. Bock has written:

> When we read any written document, we need to know what type of document it is. Is it a mystery novel, a comedy, fiction or non-fiction? Knowing the type helps us understand what is being said. This preface indicates what we are reading and why it was written. The ancients, just like us moderns, knew the difference between history and fiction. A check of [Greco-Roman] historians like Lucian, Josephus, and Thucydides indicate how well they knew their task (*e.g.*, Lucian's *How to Write History*, 39-40). The Gospel of Luke is narrative history. Although the author chooses, summarizes, and arranges how to present the events recorded, the account is an attempt to chronicle what happened nonetheless. Just as a horror film will have eerie music in the background to identify the nature of the scene, so this preface tells us what kind of story we are reading — an authentic portrait of Jesus.[3]

Nevertheless, there are those who still question Luke's reliability and credibility, saying that his theological commitments led to his "creative and imaginative" redaction of his sources. But those who have carefully investigated this matter have found that Luke does not engage in any editing or arranging of his source material that was not sanctioned by the canons of Greco-Roman historiography. Nor does he redact his sources so as to teach anything they did not clearly teach or imply in their original form. In their book, *The Riddle of the New Testament*, New Testament scholars Hoskyns and Davey make an exhaustive comparison of both Matthew and Luke's use of Mark, which is generally considered the first of the Gospels to be written, and come to the following conclusion:

> The authors of the later gospels are concerned for their Greek readers. They add, in order to make clear what Jesus demands of his disciples. They simplify, in order to avoid crude misunderstanding. They omit what appears to be trivial and unnecessary. They order and arrange the tradition, in order that it may be more easily read in public or private, and they improve the grammar and style, in order that their intelligent readers may not be unreasonably provoked. But in the whole of this process of editing, they nowhere heighten Mark's tremendous conception. No deifying of a prophet or of a mere preacher of righteousness can be detected.[4]

And as for Luke's faithful adherence to the canons of ancient Greco-Roman historiography, Martin Hengel, in his book *Acts and the History of the Earliest Christianity*, has done an exhaustive study of Luke/Acts, noting that just like other historians of antiquity, Luke sometimes abbreviates, omits, elaborates or repeats when he writes. But he does not engage in any historiographical practice that cannot also be found in Josephus, Lucian, or Tacitus:

> All this editing can be found in the secular histories of Greek and Roman antiquity. On the other hand, one can hardly accuse Luke of simply having invented events, created scenes out of nothing and depicted them on a broad canvas, deliberately falsifying his traditions in an unrestrained way for a cheap effect. He is quite

certainly not simply concerned with pious edification at the expense of truth. He is not just an "edifying writer," but a historian and a theologian who needs to be taken seriously. His account always remains within the limits of what was considered reliable by the standards of antiquity.[5]

While all the other New Testament writers also followed the canons of rhetoric and historiography, in these articles I have focused mainly on Luke because he was the close friend and missionary coworker of the apostle Paul, who also shared Paul's view of the inclusivity of the Gospel, as well as his theology of grace. Furthermore, Luke provides a historical and social context in which the teaching of most of the Pauline epistles, written before AD 62, can be better interpreted and applied. For in these writings, Luke explains how a despised Messianic movement among the Jews became a worldwide religious movement that shook the foundations of the Greco-Roman empire; how Jesus inaugurated a kingdom that blessed and elevated women, the poor, and the socially marginalized; inaugurated the age of the Spirit, as foretold by Joel the prophet, when age, race, gender and social status were no longer a valid limitation on who ministered God's Word; and that Jesus, through the Spirit-filled and gifted members of his body, the church, still carries on his work of redemption and reconciliation until his second coming. These are the themes he clearly shares with the apostle Paul and which they both agree on.

Now, in our next chapter, we will look at some misrepresentations of egalitarian views of Scripture's inspiration, infallibility, and authority, then we will deal with misconceptions regarding the Protestant principle of Sola Scriptura, which some hierarchical-complementarians illegitimately use as arguments against egalitarians and their view of Scripture's teaching about men and women partnering in Christian ministry and leadership.

End Notes

1. J. G. Dunn, "The Historicity of the Synoptic Gospels," *Crisis in Christology*, p. 201.

2. John R. Edwards, "Who Do Scholars Say That I Am?" *Christianity Today*, Mar. 4, 1996, pp. 16-19.

3. Darrell Bock, "Introduction," Luke: *NIV Application Commentary*, p. 44.

4. Craig Blomberg, "Who Was Jesus? Modern Myths vs. Bible Basics, *Focal Point*, Winter 1996, pp.15-21.

5. Ibid, pp.19-20.

Misrepresentations, Corrections, and Proper Interpretation

In the last chapter, we concluded our discussion as to why the New Testament writers were to be regarded as trustworthy chroniclers and interpreters of the story of Jesus and the early church. And much of what I have presented and argued so far would present little, if any, problems to any evangelical Christian holding an egalitarian, or hierarchical-complementarian, viewpoint regarding men and women in Christian ministry and leadership. But once any egalitarian begins reasoning from Scripture (Acts 2, Gal. 3:26-4:7; 1 Cor. 12-14; and 2 Cor. 5:11-6:2) that in the new age inaugurated by the coming of the Lord Jesus Christ and the Holy Spirit, no one can be barred from full participation in Christian ministry and leadership on the sole basis of age, gender, race, or social status, watch out! Then hackles rise on the neck, and the shouts of "liberal feminist heretics" start. So we will begin by addressing the misrepresentation of our view regarding the inspiration, authority, and interpretation of the Bible.

Misrepresentations of the Egalitarian View of Scripture's Inspiration and Authority

Because we disagree with their interpretation of Scripture, some hierarchical-complementarians, will say that we do not really believe in the full inspiration, inerrancy, and infallibility of Scripture. However, those who say this have forgotten their recent church history. During the 1980's, when the "Battle for the Bible" was fierce among Christians, the International Council of Biblical Inerrancy was formed by concerned Evangelicals to uphold this high view of Scripture. Many Evangelicals, both hierarchical-complementarian and egalitarian, actively supported

ICBI. And for those who desire the information, we will briefly explain the common view of Biblical inspiration, inerrancy, and infallibility upheld and promoted by ICBI and all its supporters.

First, there is the matter of "inspiration." Most orthodox, evangelical Christians understand inspiration as that supernatural influence of the Holy Spirit, whereby the sacred writers were divinely supervised in their production of Scripture, being restrained from error and guided in the choice of words that they used, consistent with their own disparate personalities and stylistic peculiarities. The Spirit's influence and supervision involved not only concepts and ideas, but the choice of appropriate words; in their choice of essential grammatical and syntactical relationships; and according to their historical/cultural milieu, in the choice of the literary genres best suited to communicate the ideas and concepts the biblical authors desired and intended their original readers to grasp and understand. And again, while every word, sentence structure, and genre form was utilized under the Holy Spirit's influence and supervision, yet the Spirit did so without violating any writer's unique personality and writing style. This view of inspiration is designated as *the verbal, plenary inspiration of Scripture,* and commonly supported by these New Testament texts: 2 Timothy 3:14-17; 2 Peter 1:16-21; John 12:44-50; 14:9-11, 23-26; 1 Corinthians 2:6-16; 14:36-39; 1 Timothy 5:17-18; and 2 Peter 3:14-16.

Second, by "inerrancy," most orthodox, evangelical Christians mean that the entire corpus of Scripture, as originally written and published by the prophets and apostles, contain neither errors of fact (material errors), nor internal contradictions (formal errors). Inerrancy, properly speaking, is attributed only to the *autographa,* or original writings of Scripture, when they were edited and published in the final form approved by the original authors and their associates. Indeed, this had been the predominant view of biblical inerrancy held by all branches of orthodox Christianity up until the nineteenth century, when liberal critics began challenging this view. For example, in their correspondence discussing the problems connected with Bible translation and interpretation, Augustine had written to Jerome these words about apparent contradictions: "I decide that either the copied text is corrupt, or the translator did not follow what was really said in the [original] text, or that I failed to understand it." Later, in Puritan England, on this same issue Richard Baxter, Anglican pastor and theologian, also stated, "There is no error or contradiction in Scripture, but what is [found] in some copies, by failures of preservers, transcribers, printers, and translators." And then Samuel Wakefield, the great 19th century Methodist pastor and theologian, wrote regarding this matter: "But if it is once granted that they, the Scriptures, are in the least degree alloyed with error, an opening is made for every imaginable corruption. And to admit that the sacred writers were only occasionally inspired, would involve us in the greatest perplexity, because, not knowing when they were or were not inspired, we could not determine what parts of their writings should be regarded as the infallible Word of God."[1]

Now, the underlying presupposition of this evangelical view of biblical inerrancy is this: If the Bible is indeed the inspired Word of the unchanging God of grace and truth who never lies (cf. Num. 23:19 and Jas. 1:16-18), then, as of logical necessity, Scripture must also be inerrant and infallible in all that it truly teaches about the Triune God; about God's works of creation, providence, and redemption; about the life, death, and resurrection of Jesus Christ, etc. Otherwise, how could we confidently accept it as God's written Word, the final rule of all Christian belief and practice? And even though "inerrancy" pertains primarily to "the autographs," the fact that we do not possess them does not negate the inerrancy of the original New Testament text. Most evangelical New Testament scholars, whether egalitarians or hierarchical-complementarians, would agree that such is the quality of the textual evidence for the New Testament that, following the standard canons of textual criticism, the "original" New Testament text can be reconstructed from the various textual sources available (*i.e.,* ancient Greek manuscripts, ancient translations and versions, patristic writings) to within 99% certainty. And the remaining doubtful 1% does not adversely affect any New Testament doctrine essential for salvation.[2]

Third, by "infallibility," most orthodox, evangelical Christians mean that Scripture, because it is the inspired and inerrant Word of God, is a reliable and trustworthy source of truth. Therefore, it cannot itself mislead or deceive anyone who truly understands and lives by its teaching though, as Peter warns us, false teachers can and do distort the teaching of the Scriptures (*cf.* 2 Pet. 3:15-16). And, most evangelical Christians would argue, its true teaching can be known and understood by anyone who makes the effort to learn and consistently use the proper methods of biblical interpretation, which have been derived from the Scriptures themselves. As a whole, the Scriptures are clear enough and coherent enough that anyone, who will make an earnest effort to read and study it, using the historical-cultural-grammatical method of interpretation, can understand and appropriate the Bible's central message of redemption through Jesus Christ. But, admittedly, some texts are harder to understand than others, and so if these difficult texts are divorced from their proper historical, cultural, and literary context, their meaning and significance will most certainly be misunderstood and misapplied. As one Bible teacher plainly put it, "Any text without its proper context is nothing but a pretext." If we quote verses and passages without any reference to their contexts, we will miss or misread these texts' true, infallible message. So this is the predominant view regarding Biblical inspiration, inerrancy, and infallibility among a majority of orthodox, evangelical Christians, both egalitarians and hierarchical-complementarians. This takes us back to our discussion about the history of ICBI and egalitarian support of and involvement in its activities.

During the years that ICBI promoted its "high view" of Scripture, there were three major "sessions," or conferences, where debates were held regarding the inerrancy and infallibility of Scripture, the historical and cultural interpretation of Scripture, and the proper application of ancient Scripture in the modern world. And no one, whether hierarchical-complementarian or egalitarian, who disagreed with the ICBI statement regarding the full inspiration, inerrancy, and infallibility of Scripture was allowed to give a presentation. Well, there were several egalitarians that participated in these sessions and presented papers, which were included in three books printed by Zondervan. Among the egalitarians present and named in the ICBI publications were Millard J. Erickson, Gretchen Gaebelein Hull, Alan F. Johnson, Roger Nicole, and Walter C. Kaiser, Jr. If you don't believe me, then check the historical records; the original supporters of the ICBI Statement included several egalitarians.

So the plain truth is that we egalitarians really do believe the Bible is the inspired, inerrant, and infallible Word of God, the only rule by which Christian doctrine and practice must finally be measured and judged. We claim biblical support for our view of men and women as equals and partners in Christian ministry and leadership, not because we don't believe the Bible is God's written Word, but precisely because we do! We also believe that when the Bible is properly interpreted, according to the internal keys the Holy Spirit himself incorporated into Scripture, the Bible does indeed support our view of this debated issue. For we thoroughly agree with this statement by the evangelical theologian, David F. Wells: "It is dangerous to assert that God the Holy Spirit inspired the Scriptures, but somehow omitted to give us the key(s) to understand them! Systems of understanding are legitimate and proper to the extent that they arise from the Biblical Word and are themselves disciplined by it. No one can legitimately impose a foreign system on God's Word. If we do not assert the right of Scripture to stand in an authoritative relationship to every presupposition, custom, and tradition; to every teaching, practice, and ecclesiastical organization, then that authority will be co-opted either by an ecclesiastical magisterium or by a scholarly one."[3]

Misrepresentations of the Egalitarian View of Sola Scriptura and Proper Biblical Interpretation

Some misrepresentations of our view, though very clever and subtle, are deliberate and designed to undermine our credibility and integrity. For example, some hierarchical-complementarians will say that while we hold a generally high view of Scripture, when it comes to the issue of the proper relationship between men and women, we either ignore or refuse to accept "the clear teaching of Scripture." Our response to this is, "Clear to whom and on what basis? And by what method of interpretation are we supposed to arrive at this 'clear teaching'? By one actually derived from Scripture, as a whole, or by a foreign system imposed on Scripture giving some viewpoint an advantage over another?" Assuming a traditional interpretation of Scripture, and the actual teaching of Scripture, are one and the same, does not of necessity make it so; and this is true of any doctrinal dispute. For example, I have some Baptist friends who are staunch dispensationalists, who firmly believe that dispensationalism is "the clear teaching of God's Word," and so will argue that anyone who questions or disbelieves it must be a heretic. Yet, even though I myself am an historical premillennialist, I know that this is actually a question about proper interpretation of prophetic Scripture. It is not, nor ever has been, simply a matter of a heretical, liberal denial of what is "the clear teaching" of Old Testament prophecy. For anyone who insists that it is, this reveals either their ignorance of proper biblical and theological interpretation, or the prejudicial bias of their own pet interpretation. And that goes for the present issue under discussion as well.

Another ploy of our opponents is to accuse us of having no regard for the Protestant principle of *Sola Scriptura*. If this means that we do not endorse simple "proof-texting" to support one's position on some doctrinal, ethical, or socio-political issue, then we are guilty as charged. But perhaps we need to define what this principle of *Sola Scriptura* truly is and is not, so as to dispel prevalent misconceptions. So let us consider the following three points.

First of all, *Sola Scriptura* does not mean all truth can only be found in Scripture. There are many truths of mathematics, history, science, and medicine, for example, which are not found specifically in Scripture. And all such truths, if indeed true and not mistaken human notions, must cohere with the Bible's true teachings. Regarding this, Robert Bowman, Jr., has stated,

> Sometimes our knowledge of the Bible will lead us to correct our mistaken notions about history, science or psychology. On the other hand, sometimes advances in our knowledge of these fields will force us to reexamine and refine, even correct our understanding of the Bible. This happened, for example, when Galileo proved the earth revolves around the sun and therefore that the earth moves, contrary to the standard interpretations of the Bible of that time. The motto, "All truth is God's truth," is itself true. Granted sometimes people accept as true theories and speculations that are not, but that is an abuse. A simplistic "Bible-only" application of this Protestant principle that refuses to allow such corrections to our understanding

of Scripture is destructive, in two ways. First, it divides Christians, because those who are open to all truth will not allow themselves to be held back by those who are closed to anything that will not fit their set interpretations of the Bible. Second, it hampers evangelism, because intelligent non-Christians can see that such "Bible-only" fundamentalism blinds its adherents to proven truth, and this discourages them from taking Christianity seriously.[4]

Secondly, *Sola Scriptura* does not support any idea that the meaning and significance of any biblical text is always self-evident, nor that the Bible is so self-interpreting as to render how others have understood and explained Scripture as not being of any value or interest now. After all, the Jehovah's Witnesses affirm a belief in an inspired, inerrant, and infallible Bible that is the only rule for religious belief and practice. Nevertheless, they openly affirm and propagate the Arian view of Christ and the Trinity. Thus, it would appear that mere affirmation of a high view of Scripture and a bare appeal to *Sola Scriptura* guarantees neither orthodoxy nor unanimity of doctrine. Indeed, the current debate between evangelical egalitarians and hierarchical-complementarians about the eternal subordination of the Son to the Father is a clear case of this very thing. Both groups as a whole, despite what extremists on either side might say, have a high view of Scripture's inspiration and authority. What we strongly disagree about is how certain texts regarding both the relationship between the persons of the Triune God and between men and women, are to be properly interpreted and applied. Nothing more and nothing less is the real issue between us.

Thirdly, *Sola Scriptura* does not deny the necessary distinctions that must be made between the original author's intended meaning and purpose in a text, and our own interpretation and application of the text today. E. D. Hirsch explains this distinction in terms of interpretation and criticism, but the principle applies as well to biblical exegesis and exposition:

> Interpretation is the construction of textual meaning as such; it explicates (*legt aus*) those meanings, and only those meanings, which the text explicitly or implicitly represents. Criticism, on the other hand, builds on the results of interpretation; it confronts textual

meaning not as such, but as a component of a larger context...The object of interpretation is textual meaning in and for itself and may be called the meaning of the text. The object of criticism, on the other hand, is that meaning in its bearing on something else (standards of value, present concerns, etc.), and this object may therefore be called the *significance* of the text.[5]

Indeed, all biblical scholars would affirm and maintain these distinctions made by Hirsch in their practice of interpretation and exposition, even though they are interdependent processes. However, good interpretation and application must also be distinguished from erroneous or bad interpretation and application.

"When a person speaks or writes, another has to give meaning to the words, that is, interpret them...There is only good, partial, poor or erroneous interpretation. This means that everyone who seeks to expound 1 Timothy 2:8-14, or any other text, is giving their interpretation of the words written on the page...The concept of uninterpreted communication is as meaningful as a round square. No one can claim that what they say or think a communication means is the only possibility; that they alone know the fullness of meaning of what was said or written."[6]

And so in the next installment of our series, we will further consider this matter of properly interpreting and applying the teaching of Scripture.

Conclusion: Our View of Scripture and Paul's High View Are One

So the conclusion to be drawn from what we have said is this: While the Scriptures are always the *supreme* authority for all Christian belief and practice, yet they must be read, interpreted, and applied in accordance with the interpretative tradition (*i.e.* the historical-cultural-grammatical method) that has been passed on to us by our Christian forebears. If we do not read, interpret, and apply the Bible in this way, then we will fail to distinguish the true teaching of God's Word from the clever and deceptive teachings of men. However, the main point of the present article has been to pound the final nail in the coffin for the charges often made that egalitarians have a low view of the inspiration, infallibility and authority of Scripture, and so do not truly or consistently practice *Sola Scriptura*, and so lay this body of false charges to rest once and for all. For our view of Scripture is one with that of the apostle Paul and so is a "high view" of Scripture: "All Scripture is inspired by God and is useful to teach us what is true and to make us realize what is wrong in our lives. It corrects us when we are wrong and teaches us to do what is right. God uses it to prepare and equip his people to do every good work" (2 Tim. 3:16-17, NLT).

End Notes

1. All three quotes from John D. Woodbridge's *Biblical Authority: A Critique of the Rogers/McKim Proposal*, Zondervan Publishers, 1982.

2. Daniel B. Wallace, "Inerrancy and the Text of the New Testament," *Evidence for God*, Edited by William A. Dembski and Michael R. Licona, pp.211-219.

3. David F. Wells, "The Bible, Doctrine, and Theological Contextualization," *The Use of the Bible in Theology*, p. 187.

4. Robert Bowman, Jr. *Orthodoxy and Heresy: A Biblical Guide to Doctrinal Discernment*, pp.100-101.

5. E.D. Hirsch. "Appendix 1: Objective Interpretation," *Validity In Interpretation*, pp. 210-211.

6. Kevin Giles, *Response to the Melbourne Hierarchical-Complementarians*, p.13.

Issues Regarding Interpretation and Application of Scripture

In chapter five, we ended with a discussion on issues connected with the Protestant principle of *Sola Scriptura* and the proper interpretation and application of Scripture. And there we made two simple but very important points: A firm belief in the inspiration, inerrancy, and infallibility of Scripture is no guarantee, in and of itself, that one will also hold and teach the orthodox view of Christ, the Trinity, and other key Christian doctrines. Nor is a simplistic "the Bible-only" understanding of *Sola Scriptura*, that is not grounded in generally accepted standards of biblical exegesis and theological interpretation, a guarantee that the essential doctrines and life principles of the Christian faith are going to be effectively proclaimed and defended.

The Relationship between Traditions and Sola Scriptura Clarified

Indeed, the real problem with this simplistic understanding of *Sola Scriptura* is its disdain for historical theological tradition of any kind, often branding such tradition as "the traditions of men" which are worthless, never making the proper distinction between scripturally warranted and unwarranted traditions. And yet I can say with confidence that in the fundamentalist Baptist church I grew up in, when it came to such issues as the order of worship, the dispensational understanding of Old Testament prophecy, and the special gifts of the Holy Spirit being available today (just to mention a few), what was taught and upheld as true and right on these issues was more a matter of "our Baptist heritage and tradition" than what the Bible was actually known to teach and demand on these issues.

When I went to Bible college and learned more about proper biblical exegesis and theological interpretation, I discovered that some things that I had been taught as "gospel truths" were strictly rooted in "our Baptist heritage and tradition," and not necessarily in the teaching of Scripture itself; rather it was a particular interpretation being passed off as "the clear teaching" of the Bible. I also learned that Scripture made a distinction between the "false traditions of men" which contradicted what Scripture itself actually taught and demanded of God's people (*cf.* Matt. 15:1-9), and the true "apostolic tradition" which summarized actual truths and life principles of the gospel and which were passed on to the churches by Paul and the other apostles to help them distinguish truth from error (*cf.* 1 Cor. 11:1 and 2 Tim. 1:13-14). So I discovered that the Protestant principle of *Sola Scriptura* is not necessarily opposed to certain common historical and theological traditions held in common by Catholic, Protestant, and Eastern Orthodox Christians. As Robert Bowman, Jr. explains:

> [*Sola Scriptura*] does not mean all traditions are based on falsehood. Traditions that cannot be found in the Bible are not thereby proved false. To prove a tradition false, it must be shown to *contradict* the Bible. If this cannot be done, then the tradition must be evaluated on the basis of the historical evidence for its authenticity. For example, the Bible never identifies explicitly any of the authors of the four Gospels. However, that does not invalidate the traditions that they were written by Matthew, Mark, Luke and John. On the other hand, traditions that cannot be substantiated from the Bible should not be made binding on Christians. That is, Christians should not be required to accept as dogmas traditions that do not have [clear] biblical warrant.[1]

Furthermore, there are many traditional readings of various Scripture texts that, though having had a long history and having been held by various Christian writers, did not have clear and unquestionable Scriptural warrant and so were not incorporated in the ecumenical creeds and Reformed confessions of faith, which means that even though many might still hold such views, they cannot be regarded as, or required as, dogmas that all Christians must embrace as either necessary for salvation or for living a life pleasing to God. These may be considered "weak" interpretative traditions, while those rooted in the Scriptures and which the church has recognized and incorporated in its historical creeds and confessions are "strong" interpretative traditions and do serve as reliable aids in interpreting and applying Scripture.

Indeed, in the current debate on the Trinity, this distinction between "strong" and "weak" interpretative traditions has been made by Kevin Giles:

> As horrified as [Wayne] Grudem might be that I said in *The Trinity and Subordinationism* that on the Trinity and other doctrinal issues the Bible can be read in more than one way, I stand by what I said. I think my assertion is irrefutable. He and I do not agree on how the Bible should be read on the Trinity. He holds that all comments that speak of the subordination of the Son in the incarnation should be read back into the immanent (ontological) Trinity, and I take the opposite position. Athanasius and those he designated "Arians" also disagreed on exactly the same issue. Much of Athanasius' "Discourses Against the Arians" are taken up with his interpretation of passages the Arians interpreted to support the eternal subordination of the Son in being, function, and authority. One of the painful things evangelicals must honestly face is that a high view of Scripture does not necessarily lead to unanimity in doctrine...This is where tradition is so important. Over the centuries a way of reading the Bible on key matters has emerged, and in the case of the Trinity and Christology, this way has been codified in the ecumenical creeds. This agreed interpretation of Scripture, which is called "the tradition," is not of equal authority with Scripture. It is a secondary authority not to be ignored, particularly so when codified in creeds and confessions, yet always subject to the correction of Scripture. The Reformers held to exactly the same high view of the interpretative tradition and had the same low regard for "church tradition" as I do...For the Reformers the best guide to rightly interpreting Scripture was the work of those who had carefully studied and debated its meaning before them...On the Trinity, we will show in what follows that what [Grudem] teaches is directly in opposition to what the best theologians of the past

and the creeds teach. In regard to the subordination of women, the situation is not the same. Both he and I have in fact broken with the "weak tradition" that spoke uniformly for eighteen centuries of the "inferiority" of women and the "superiority" of men, and of women being more prone to sin and error.[2]

Unlike the doctrine of the Trinity, which was thoroughly studied, debated and then affirmed at the Council of Nicaea, as regards the "weak" tradition of "superior" men ruling "inferior" women, we have an entirely different situation. No body of Christians, composed by the best thinkers and scholars, has ever formerly come together to fully study, debate, and then by Spirit-directed consensus, formulate a doctrinal statement regarding the biblical and orthodox view of women and men in Christian leadership and ministry to which all Christians agree and subscribe. And while hierarchists maintain that their understanding of "equal in being and yet different in function and authority," as regards both men and women and the persons of the Trinity, is both the biblical and traditional view, the plain fact is that, not only do a number of other orthodox, evangelical Christians dispute their viewpoint, but there is no universally agreed upon doctrinal statement to which they can appeal, nor one to which all Christians agree and willingly subscribe.

Nor does their "equal in being yet different in function and authority" doctrine sit well with the teaching of the Nicene and Athanasian creeds. My own studies in the historical development and exposition of the Trinity revealed that while there have been a few theologians who argued for some form of subordination within the Godhead, the majority of them — as represented by Athanasius, Augustine, Calvin, and Warfield — have argued that the Father, Son, and Spirit are coeternal and coequal in their divine being, attributes, rank, power, authority, and glory. Indeed, they agree with the pronouncement made at the Council of Rome in AD 382, "If anyone denies that the Father, Son, and Holy Spirit have one divinity, authority, majesty, power, one glory, dominion, one kingdom, and one will and truth; he is a heretic. If anyone denies that the three persons, the Father, the Son, and the Holy Spirit, are true persons, equal, eternal, containing all things visible and invisible, that they are omnipotent, judge all things, give life to all things, make all things, and conserve all things; he is a heretic." And in the Augustinian-Calvinistic tradition I come from, the primary operations and roles of the Father, Son, and Spirit in the works of creation, providence, and redemption are not rooted in a hierarchy of authority among the divine persons, but in a mutual agreement or covenant between them to take these up as their primary function and work, while still working together in full unity and harmony of mind, power, and will to accomplish the eternal purposes of the one triune God.

Quite frankly, I am convinced that the hierarchists' view is a hybrid of the "weaker" tradition, mixed with elements of pagan Greek "chain of being" theory and nineteenth century social theory. So when I'm told by some of these hierarchists that their view is "the clear teaching of Scripture and of the church's theological tradition," and knowing what I do about the history and nature of biblical and theological interpretation, I am very skeptical, to say the least. At this point, I find myself in full agreement with Gordon Fee as to what constitutes a normative Christian theology:

> [A] theology that articulates what all Christians in all places and at all times should believe needs to be drawn from [biblical] texts that teach such theology explicitly or from texts where the theology is implicitly embedded in what is being said. But in the latter instances, such theology should also reflect the universal perspective of Scripture, without ambiguity and diverse witness. Where there is ambiguity and diversity of witness, it would seem that what is being "taught" is Christian truth that is being accommodated to that culture and its structures.[3]

As regards some biblical texts used by our hierarchical friends, I believe there is a failure on their part to adequately distinguish the eternal truth or principle being taught from its historical and cultural accommodation and application. I do not believe their view reflects "the universal perspective of Scripture" as a whole, nor does it reflect the "universal perspective" of the Pauline writings in particular, precisely because it fails to deal honestly with the "ambiguity and diversity of witness" found in the Scripture.

But, once again, this confirms that the *Sola Scriptura* principle is not mere "proof-texting" to support our differing viewpoints on various theological, moral, or socio-political issues. Rather it recognizes that while the Scriptures are the supreme authority, yet they must be read, interpreted, and applied in accordance with the interpretative tradition drawn that has been passed on to us by our Christian forebears. It is only as we read, interpret, and apply the Bible in this way that we will distinguish the true teaching of Scripture from the clever and deceptive teachings of men. And so in the section that follows, I want to outline what I perceive as five key elements of that interpretative tradition.

The Five Key Elements of Biblical Interpretation

1. *Scripture has to be understood in terms of its own historical, cultural and literary context before the modern interpreter can grasp the text's true significance and application to modern intellectual, moral and socio-political issues.* Any text read and applied apart from its context is nothing more than some pretext for a conservative, liberal, or secular agenda unrelated to the teaching of Scripture itself. "It is necessary for us to take seriously the historical context of any given passage and of the Bible as a whole...Much misinterpretation has resulted from disregard for the historical context of the passage to be interpreted. A study of the Bible is always a study of a people. It is necessary therefore to enter the world of the Hebrew people and the people of the early church. This includes understanding their ways of thinking, their cultural pattern, and their distinctiveness amid the surrounding cultures and nations." [4]

2. *The whole testimony of Scripture must be taken into account when examining any doctrinal, ethical, or socio-political issue.* Obscure portions of Scripture are to be explained by the clearer portions, with the overall spirit of the total teaching of Scripture serving as the final arbiter of the correct meaning, significance, and application of the individual text under consideration. "One of the major errors in biblical interpretation is the failure to relate a given passage of Scripture to the overall message of Scripture. It is therefore necessary to take seriously the message of the Bible as a whole and compare Scripture with Scripture. This requires acquaintance with the unfolding drama of the Bible, its

major themes, and how the various themes are related and integrated into a whole."⁵

3. *A text or portion of Scripture must be interpreted and applied appropriately according to its intended main emphasis as confirmed by the immediate or larger context of Scripture, and never for any attendant features.* For example, prior to the American Civil War, various Christians who defended the institution of slavery argued: Since Abraham was a man of faith and a friend of God who was never censured for being a slave-owner, then one could own slaves without losing his good standing as a Christian, provided he was a benevolent slave master like Abraham. But the real question to ask was, "Is it proper and right to use the life of Abraham to defend the institution of slavery?" If so, Mormons and other sects, both then and now, ask on what grounds they are being punished for their practice of concubinage and polygamy. If Abraham and the other patriarchs, as men of faith approved by God, were not censured for their practice of concubinage and polygamy, then why were they being condemned and punished for doing what these Old Testament saints were permitted to do? Therefore, instead of using these patriarchal narratives to defend slavery and polygamy, they should be used, as the author of Hebrews indicates in Chapter 11, to show how the testing of Abraham's faith in God and his promises, is to serve as an example of the Christian's call to a life of steadfastness and faithfulness.

4. *The fourth principle is that of typological or analogical/messianic interpretation.* This rule not only incorporates the concept that the relationship between the Old and New Testaments is one of promise and fulfillment, but also that of analogical typology between key Old Testament persons, events, and religious institutions with the Lord Jesus Christ and his church in their joint redemptive mission, which has inaugurated the present and yet future kingdom of God that awaits the second coming for its full, glorious manifestation in the world. In fact, the mainstream of biblical scholarship now recognizes that typology expresses the basic hermeneutic, indeed the attitude or perspective, by which both Old Testament and New Testament writers understood themselves and their predecessors. "Each new community in the ongoing development of salvation history viewed itself analogously in terms of the past. This is true within the OT as well as in

the NT use of the OT. The two major sources, of course, were creation and the Exodus. Creation typology is especially seen in Rom. 5 and the Adam-Christ parallel, while Exodus or covenantal typology predominates in both testaments. Positively, the Exodus was behind the redemptive imagery in Isa. 51-52 as well as NT salvific concepts (*e.g.*, 1 Cor. 10:1-6). Negatively, the wilderness wanderings became the model for future admonition (*e.g.*, Ps. 95:7-8; Heb. 4:3-11)."[6]

5. *The fifth principle is that of the Pauline eschatological rule of the new creation/ new age,* which is clearly set forth in such Pauline texts as Romans 4:13-17; 8:9-25; 1 Corinthians 12:12-27; 2 Corinthians 5:11-6:2; Galatians 3:26-4:7 and Ephesians 2:11-22. According to this biblical/theological rule, Paul teaches that through "the Christ event" — *i.e.*, by means of Jesus Christ's life, death, resurrection, and his pouring out of the Holy Spirit on the church — the eschatological promise of the Abrahamic covenant is realized at the end of the old age, which is passing away at the dawning of the new age inaugurated by the first advent of Christ and which awaits his second coming for its full realization. And this fulfillment of the Abrahamic covenant, both in Christ and those united with him, who is "the seed of Abraham'" — *i.e.*, "the new humanity" and body of Christ, made up of all who are united with Christ by faith, who all have received the new covenant sign of baptism, who all live by the law of Christ, who all have been renewed and baptized into that body by the one Spirit who gifts and calls all followers of Christ to works of ministry — results in all believers lovingly worshipping God and serving humanity as did Christ, the Son of God and the son of Abraham.

"It is especially difficult for most of us to imagine the effect of Paul's [teaching] in a culture where position and status preserved order through basically uncrossable boundaries. Paul asserts that when people come into the fellowship of Christ Jesus, significance is no longer to be found in being Jew or Greek, slave or free, male or female. The all-embracing nature of this affirmation, its counter-cultural significance, the fact that it *equally disadvantages all* by *equally advantaging all* — these stand at the very heart of a culture sustained by people maintaining the right position and status. But in Christ Jesus, the One whose death and resurrection inaugurated the new creation, all things have become new; the new era has dawned. The new creation, therefore, must be our starting point regarding gender issues, because this is theologically where Paul lived. Everything else he says comes out of this worldview of what has happened in the coming of Christ in the Spirit."[7]

Of course, this principle brings together three key aspects of Paul's proclamation and explanation that God was in Christ, reconciling both creation and humanity to himself (2 Cor. 5:11-6:2), and if they are not held together in proper unity and harmonious balance, then Paul's teaching on salvation in Christ, new life in the Spirit, the gifting and calling of Christians to ministry, and the nature and mission of the church is distorted into something that Paul would neither recognize nor approve of as "the gospel faith" we are both to guard and contend for with the help of the Holy Spirit (*Cf.* (Phil. 1:27-28 and 2 Tim. 1:13-14) . As Ralph Martin explains in *Reconciliation: A Study of Paul's Theology*,

> Paul's thought can best be captured in the omnibus term "reconciliation"...[as] organizing principle that will do some justice at least to three aspects of Paul's theology and religious experience. *The first* is the cosmic predicament that in some mysterious way entailed the disorder of nature, the opposition of demonic "principalities and powers," and man's need as alienated and disconsolate "sinner," bereft in the universe and estranged from a holy God. *Secondly,* the saving action of God in Jesus Christ is directed to a process of restoration that will one day lead to a reclaimed universe at one with its Creator. The sign and pledge of that cosmic renewal have already been given in what was taking place in the apostolic community— deliverance from demonic forces, the forgiveness of sins and life in the fellowship of the Spirit under the Lordship of the exalted Christ. One token in particular was evidence of the new age that, it was believed, had dawned with the post-Easter triumph of Christ and his new life in the Spirit. Barriers of separation were being broken down, not only between God and the sinful race of humankind, but just as impressively between the inveterately distanced groups in ancient society: Jew/Gentile; slave/free; male/female. Life in the

society of the new creation, the church, was a marker of what God was accomplishing in the world at large, and this revolution in the microcosm of the church was treated as a foretaste and promise of God's plan to embrace the whole cosmos in his new order. *Thirdly, Paul's own experience which dated from his encounter with the living Lord became a transcript from which he read off a major part of his theology, viz. the reconciliation and pacification of the world...* He both rejoiced in the new status of friendship and amity that was his following his conversion, and went on to express the role of the church as a reconciling agent in God's design. The prospect of the church's mission is couched in terms embracing the entire world, of which the coming to existence of a new community in the church was a pledge. It only needed the letter to the Ephesians to elaborate and develop the teaching in order to produce a well-rounded philosophy of history in which cosmic reconciliation is the achieved goal.[8]

Conclusion: The Real Bone of Contention

My friends, let us be clear on one thing: when all the white noise in the debate between egalitarians and hierarchical-complementarians is filtered out, it soon becomes clear what the real bone of contention is between us. It is not about the inspiration, infallibility, and authority of Scripture, nor a different understanding and practice of the *Sola Scriptura* principle, *contra* the assertions made by our opponents. No, it is all about this fifth interpretative principle derived from Paul's own writings, and its thorough and consistent application, that separate us. And it is long past time that hierarchical-complementarians admitted that this is the case.

Endnotes

1. Robert Bowman, Jr., *Orthodoxy and Heresy: A Biblical Guide to Doctrinal Discernment*, pp. 61-62.

2. Kevin Giles, "Getting Things Straight: The Issues in Contention," *Jesus and the Father: Modern Evangelicals Reinvent the Doctrine of the Trinity*, pp. 70-71.

3. Gordon Fee, "Hermeneutics and the Gender Debate," *Discovering Biblical Equality*, p. 378.

4. Willard M. Swartley, "Biblical Interpretation in the Life of the Church," *Slavery, Sabbath, War and Women: Case Issues in Biblical Interpretation*, pp. 240-241.

5. Ibid., pp. 241-242.

6. Grant R. Osborne, "Type, Typology," *The Evangelical Dictionary of Theology*, ed. Walter A. Elwell, p.1118.

7. Gordon Fee, "Gender Issues: Reflections on the Perspective of the Apostle Paul," *Listening to the Spirit in the Text*, pp. 59-61.

8. Ralph Martin, "Leading Themes," *Reconciliation: A Study of Paul's Theology*, pp.46-47.

Pneumatic-Communal Interpretation of Scripture and Conflict Resolution

In the first draft of this booklet, I had begun to discuss *pneumatic-communal interpretation* as a principle of interpretation *per se*. Then after reviewing it for possible revision and editing, I realized that it is more than that: it is the scriptural, Holy Spirit initiated and directed method for the church, as a whole, to adequately deal with divisive doctrinal and ethical disputes, to come to a mutually agreed consensus as to the truth of the matter at issue, and to restore unity and harmony to the life and mission of the church. And in seeking to communicate the nature and purpose of pnuematic-communal interpretation, I also realized that some aspects of this subject had been addressed before, in good measure, by Alice Matthews in her essay in *Discovering Biblical Equality*, "Toward Reconciliation: Healing the Schism." I am well acquainted with Alice, and years ago worked with her and Jim Beck in what was then the Front Range Chapter of CBE. She is an excellent scholar and writer, possessing wisdom and discernment, and so one can learn much from her essay. However, she wrote her article in 2005; I'm writing in 2011. Consequently, though the substance is the same, there may be some difference in our perspectives and concerns.

So let me begin with my understanding of what I will call *the pneumatic-communal rule of Scriptural interpretation and application*. This form of explaining and applying the Scriptures is based on the necessary cooperation that must exist between the Holy Spirit and the Church in settling controversies and disputes that affect the life and ministry of the whole Body of Christ. As I see it, there are several distinct but related elements that constitute this form of Biblical interpretation and application.

First, it involves the recognition by both leaders and the congregations that *the teaching and guiding ministry of the Holy Spirit did not cease* with the completion of the New Testament canon and the death of the original apostles of Christ. For the Holy Spirit is and remains, until Christ returns, the ultimate author and interpreter of Scripture. He is still present and active in the church, leading all true believers to a unified understanding of and compliance with the mind and will of the Lord Jesus Christ, the one and only head of the church, as revealed in the Scriptures which the Holy Spirit inspired (*cf.* 1 Cor. 2:6-16; 13:1-14:1; 2 Tim. 3:14-16; 1 John. 2:27, TEV).

Second, it involves the recognition that in every generation, *the Lord Jesus Christ, through the Holy Spirit, gifts and calls both men and women to be church-planters, preachers, evangelists, and pastor-teachers* (1 Cor. 12:1-14, 27-30; Eph. 4:7-11). Their responsibility is to bring Christians under their care to spiritual maturity in Christ, and to help them discover their gifts and calling. Then they must train them to be both biblically and theologically literate as well as practically competent. In this way, they will be fully equipped for the "works of service" Christ wants all his people to do within the Body and in reaching the needy world around them (1 Cor. 14:1-12; Eph. 4:8-10). But they are not to lord it over the people, denying the gifting and calling they have received from the Spirit, who gifts and calls both men and women to ministry in full agreement with the desires and choices of both the Father and Son (*cf.* 1 Pet. 5:1-4; John 16:12-15; 1 Cor. 12:4-7).

Third, it involves both leaders and people, *working together and holding each other accountable, to maintain the unity of truth, love, and righteousness which is to mark the church, the body of Christ* (*cf.* Eph. 4:1-6). Not only are leaders to help the congregation stand firm in the faith, live righteous lives, and engage in effective ministry consistent with the Spirit's gifting and calling, but the people as fellow servants of the Lord and his Word, must also rebuke the leaders when they forget they are guides and equippers, and instead seek to be lords of the congregation when there is only one Lord; or when they depart from essential Christian doctrine and start teaching their own opinions as gospel truth; or when they live such ungodly lives that Christ and the gospel are profaned because of them (*cf.* 1 Thess. 5:19-20; 1 Tim. 5:17-21; Jude 3-4).

The True Priesthood of All Believers in Practice

Now, what I am here describing as pneumatic-communal rule of interpretation is not some novel concoction of my own. Indeed, this communal method and practice of maintaining the unity and purity of the church in life, doctrine and worship is, according to Alister McGrath, what the Reformers ideally understood to be the true nature and practice of *the priesthood of all believers*, a doctrine which all Protestants claim to affirm:

> On the basis of the doctrine of the universal priesthood of believers, Luther insisted that every Christian has the right to interpret the Bible and to raise concerns about any aspect of the church's teaching or practice that appears to be inconsistent with the Bible. There is no "spiritual" authority, distinct from or superior to ordinary Christians, who can impose certain readings of the Bible upon the church. Luther clearly believed that the Bible was sufficiently clear for ordinary Christians to be able to read and understand it. Luther insisted that all believers have the right to read the Bible in a language they can understand and to interpret its meaning for themselves. The church is thus held accountable to its members for its interpretation of the sacred text and is open to challenge at every point. The significance of Luther's point can hardly be overlooked. By insisting it had a divinely ordained monopoly on biblical interpretation, the medieval church had declared itself to be above criticism on biblical grounds. No external critic had the authority to interpret Scripture and thus apply it to criticize the church's doctrines or practices. Luther's response was to empower the laity as interpreters of the Bible and to hold the church accountable to its people for what it taught. And if they were not satisfied with the outcome, they, as laity, had the right to demand a reforming council be convened to address their concerns.[1]

Now, this divinely ordained and approved method of dealing with and settling doctrinal and ethical disputes in the church has been recognized since the time the Council of Jerusalem met to debate the unity and equality of Jews and Gentiles in Christ (*cf*. Acts 15:1-35). But it has not been followed without great difficulty, and not always to the full satisfaction of every party involved, or always ending with the results some had hoped for, as Alice Mathews herself has pointed out:

> If there is to be reconciliation, it must begin with the realization that the chasm between the two sides is real and significant. We must see and respect this conflict for what it is: a struggle for truth. No one in the struggle can dismiss opponents merely by labeling them — whether as power-hungry defenders of the status quo or as pawns of contemporary culture who are willing to compromise Scripture for the sake of a social agenda. Truth is on the line for God-fearing Christians on both sides of the chasm. When we fail to respect those who hold views that call our own beliefs into question, we miss the valid and ongoing struggle for truth. But in the effort to respect those with whom we disagree, we are faced with the painful necessity of doing so without abandoning this struggle. This, of course, is not the first time in the history of the church that contrary understandings of biblical truth have faced the people of God. The great councils in the early centuries remind us that God-fearing Christians disagreed vigorously and often separated over core issues. Later, in the sixteenth century, Martin Luther opposed certain teachings and practices of the Roman Catholic Church, launching the Reformation when he nailed his ninety-nine theses to the Wittenberg door. Out of that act more than a hundred years of military warfare between Catholics and Protestants erupted in Europe. More recently, conservative Christians were divided over the issue of slavery, some using Scripture to defend the practice of owning other human beings and others using it to abolish that practice.[2]

And in the last case of the conflict between the abolitionists and the anti-abolitionists, it must be remembered that while both parties believed in an inspired, inerrant, infallible, and authoritative Bible, not only did their methods of interpretation and application differ, but they also had a completely different understanding of "salvation and freedom in Christ."

The abolitionists believed the gospel of Christ brought deliverance from sin, reconciliation with God, and spiritual renewal of believers, but also possessed intellectual and socio-political implications that called for either the reformation or overthrow of institutionalized beliefs, practices, and policies that were seen as unjust, oppressive, and dehumanizing. The anti-abolitionists understood the gospel's teaching on "salvation and freedom in Christ" strictly in terms of deliverance from sin, reconciliation with God, and direct access to God through prayer. But they did not believe that it called for any radical reform of the present social order or institutions; if anything, it enabled poor whites, slaves, and women to gladly and contentedly accept their assigned places in a patriarchal structure (*i.e.* "the order of creation") where rich and powerful white males dominated over all others.

The True Division is Hermeneutical/Theological, Not Biblical

Indeed, it is the same hermeneutical/theological problem that existed between the abolitionists and the anti-abolitionists that exists between egalitarians and hierarchical-complementarians today: a *progressive* redemptive hermeneutic vs. a *static* redemptive hermeneutic. Basically, there are two ways to read and apply Scripture: a) a progressive redemptive hermeneutic, which encourages movement beyond the original application of the text in ancient society; or b) a static approach, which understands the words of a text in isolation from their ancient historical-cultural context and with little or no emphasis on their underlying spirit. William J. Webb has dealt with this issue in terms of what he calls "The X-Y-Z Principle":

> Within [this] model, the *central position* (Y) represents particular words of the Bible at that stage of their development of a subject, if those words are understood in an isolated, "on the page" sense. On either side of the biblical text's words, one must ask the question of perspective. First, how is the text to be understood from the perspective of the *original culture* (X)? And then, what does the text look like in our culture, when our culture happens to reflect a more redemptive social ethic — closer to an *ultimate ethic* (Z) — than the ethic revealed in the culturally particularized words of the biblical text? From the one direction the biblical text appears redemptive; from the other direction it appears regressive.

And to explain the difference between these alternate ways of reading and applying the text of Scripture, Webb gives the following illustration:

> To illustrate: Deuteronomy 23:15-16 instructs Israel to provide safety and refuge to slaves fleeing harsh treatment in a foreign country. Such a slave was to be given shelter, was permitted to live in any of Israel's cities and was not to be handed over to his or her master. The redemptive dimension of this slavery legislation sparkles brightly in comparison to that of the surrounding nations. Most ancient Near Eastern countries had extradition treaties and administered severe punishment to runaway slaves, their families and those who aided in their escape.
>
> A static hermeneutic would apply this slavery-refuge text by staying strictly with the words on the page, read in isolation from their "movement" meaning. Rather than being led by the spirit-movement meaning of this text to cry out for the abolition of slavery, the static reader would permit slavery in our culture (because the Bible did)—although she or he might seek to show kindness toward runaway slaves within the church or to give refuge to slaves in abusive relationships. Such an approach to applying the Bible would emphasize the words of the text in a highly isolated sense, while missing the spirit of the text.[3]

Now, the underlying presupposition of Webb's "redemptive-movement hermeneutic" is the Pauline theological concept of the new creation, enumerated in such texts as Galatians 3:28-4:7 and 2 Corinthians 5:11-6:2, wherein the consequences of the fall, such as slavery and the dominance of men over women are, by the Christ event and the indwelling of the church by the Holy Spirit, reversed and overcome with the abolition of slavery and the mutuality of men and women in the church. However, our hierarchist friends do not share the same presupposition that we do, and so they do not consistently apply this redemptive-movement hermeneutic as we do. And until this hermeneutical/theological divide between the two parties is understood, acknowledged, and honestly dealt with, reconciliation cannot occur. Therefore I would argue, on the basis of the pneumatic-communal rule, that *in times of great doctrinal conflict and debate*, not only the leaders but also representative members of the congregations, need to come together in a "reform" council for earnest, soul-searching prayer, for careful and thorough study of what the Scriptures actually teach on the issue being discussed, while depending on the Spirit of truth to bring all to a unified understanding of God's mind and will therein revealed (*cf.* Acts 15:1-6). And after all the concerns and issues of all the parties involved in the controversy have been given a full and fair consideration—apart from any humiliation, censorship, or coercion of one party by the other—whether it be by a special "prophetic word" or not, it must be by the Holy Spirit that all come to a unified understanding and consensus as what the "true doctrine" is and how it is to be applied (*cf.* Acts 15:30-36). For only then will the unity and peace of the Church be restored; only then will all Christians joyfully and harmoniously work together; only then will the gospel of Christ, spread by a Spirit-renewed, united, and empowered church, have the transforming impact in our society and in our world that so many of us long for (*cf.* Acts 15:30-36).

What Egalitarians Must Not Concede to Hierarchists

Now, up to this point, I think Alice Mathews and I are in agreement. However, believing God has gifted me and called me to be a prophetic teacher like Barnabas, I not only see it as part of my responsibility to instruct and encourage, building up and equipping Christians in their life and work for Christ and his kingdom, but also, when necessary, to firmly stand against and speak-out against what I perceive as destructive heresies that have the potential to decimate both the life and mission of the church. So what I say in this final section may displease some readers, but I must be faithful to God and "contend for the faith God has once for all time entrusted to his holy people" (Jude 3, my rendering).

If egalitarians and hierarchists ever decide to have some kind of reconciliation conference, there are some points of disagreement that I would insist that egalitarians must not, for any reason, concede to hierarchists:

1. The doctrine of the eternal subordination of the Son. As has already been noted earlier, the orthodox view of the Trinity is that the Father, Son, and

Spirit are coeternal and coequal in their divine being, attributes, rank, power, authority, and glory. Indeed the Council of Rome in AD 382, being in full agreement with the Eastern church, declared, "If anyone denies that the Father, Son, and Holy Spirit have one divinity, authority, majesty, power, one glory, dominion, one kingdom, and one will and truth; he is a heretic. If anyone denies that the three persons, the Father, the Son, and the Holy Spirit, are true persons, equal, eternal, containing all things visible and invisible, that they are omnipotent, judge all things, give life to all things, make all things, and conserve all things; he is a heretic." Therefore, semi-Arianism being propagated by Wayne Grudem, George Knight III, John Piper, and Bruce Ware must be censured and repudiated as the false, destructive heresy that it is.[4] Consider well Shirley Guthrie's critique of their position:

> God is like a committee or board in which there is one big boss and two subordinates who go out to do what the boss orders: One God (the Father) and two "agents" of God (the Son and the Spirit) who are invested with divine power, but are still less than God. This protects the oneness of God, but at the expense of suggesting that neither the Son nor the Spirit is really God-with-us, and that there might be a conflict between what the "top God" and God's inferior "representatives" will and do (between the Father's sovereign power over and above us, the Son's self-giving love for us, and the Spirit's intimate presence within and among us, for instance).[5]

So whether these hierarchists will admit it or not, the Eternal Subordination of the Son (ESS) is a doctrine that denies the full equality of Father, Son, and Holy Spirit in divine majesty, knowledge, power, and authority. Though they blather about the reasonability of their concept of the divine persons as both equal in being and yet at the same time hierarchically structured in roles and works due to their being different persons — the truth is, as Kevin Giles, Millard Erickson, and Alan Myatt have shown[6], that if the eternal, subordinate function of the Son and Spirit define who they are in relation to the Father, and are not descriptive of what they covenanted as equals with the Father to do, then, as of logical necessity, despite the disclaimers made, the Son and Spirit are ontologically inferior to the Father. And if the Son and the Spirit are ontologically inferior to the Father, then as Athanasius, Basil, and Gregory the Theologian argued, then the Son cannot truly be our redeemer and mediator, nor the Spirit our counselor, life-giver and sanctifier; for though more God-like than angels and humans, they are not fully God in the same sense as the Father in divine majesty, knowledge, power, and authority. They cannot, on the basis of this semi-Arian teaching, fully and intimately know the Father, nor enable anyone else to so know him, which contradicts texts such as Matthew 11:27-30 and 1 Corinthians 2:6-16. Remember what the apostle John said, "Do not believe everyone who claims to speak by Spirit. You must test them to see if the spirit they have comes from God...If someone claims to be a prophet and does not acknowledge the truth about Jesus, that person is not from God" (1 John 4:1-2, 3). Therefore, I again insist that, if any reconciliation conference is held, egalitarians must stand firm and insist on the rejection and repudiation of this Trinitarian heresy.

2. *The priority of the Spirit's call and gifting to ministry.* From the doctrine of the Trinity, as defined and argued above, it follows that God's gracious ministry of redemption and reconciliation, which began to be accomplished through Christ and the Spirit, is now carried on through the church as the body of Christ, which Christ energizes, gifts, and directs by the Holy Spirit to carry on this same ministry of redemption and reconciliation (*cf.* 2 Cor. 5:11-20; Eph. 4:11-16). Indeed, the priority of the Spirit's call and gifting for ministry is rooted in the fact that while the Spirit decides "which gift each person should have" (1 Cor. 12:11, NLT), he does so in full agreement and co-operation with the Father and the Son. For as Augustine and so many others have pointed out from the Scriptures (*e.g.*, John 14:16-17; 16:12-15; 1 John 2:24-27), the three persons work together in mutual support, harmony, and co-operation in all the works of creation, providence, and reconciliation, even though they have taken certain works to be primarily their own. And so when the Spirit gifts and calls men and women to ministry, he does so both in agreement with the Father and Son and with their full approval. Here, in a short space, we arguing for the Trinitarian foundation for the priority of the Spirit's gifting and calling before any man or woman assumes to engage in any ministry or assume any position of leadership in the

church. Patrick S. Franklin, who has argued the case much more fully, states the matter as follows:

> The Holy Spirit initiates and empowers all ministries and, properly speaking, is the agent of every ministry (*e.g.*, Luke 4:14-15, 18-19; Acts 1:8; Rom. 8:26-27; 1 Cor. 12:3-11). The prior and continuing ministry of God the Father, through the Son and in the Spirit, grounds and sustains all ministry, not the intelligence, creativity, or strategic efforts of human beings, nor their innate or biological advantages (*e.g.*, John 15:26, 16:12-15, 20:21-22; 1 Cor. 2:1-5). This does not mean that human action is meaningless, but that it is always a response to God's prior working. While this response is truly our response, it is not thereby efficacious as such (Gal. 2:19-20). It becomes efficacious only through the creative, reconciling, and redeeming power of the Holy Spirit, who "commandeers" our words and actions such that our deficient language actually proclaims the Word of God and our feeble efforts actually accomplish the work of Christ. Ministry is therefore, both a response to and an abiding in grace—and grace, according to Karl Barth, is always God's deed and act...Based on the logic of Trinitarian grace,...the Father, Son, and Holy Spirit work collaboratively to draw human persons into participating in the ministry of God. This occurs as the Holy Spirit unites the prior and ongoing ministry of Christ with the responsive ministry of women and men to accomplish the will of the Father, who is the origin and destiny of all ministry.[7]

Of course, Pastor Franklin is not the first to recognize and insist that prior to anything else, those who engage in Christian ministry and leadership must be regenerate believers, specifically gifted and called by the Spirit to such ministry and leadership. During the Great Awakening of the eighteenth century, this was insisted on by a number of revival leaders and preachers such as John Wesley, George Whitefield, Jonathan Edwards, Isaac Backus, and William Law.

Isaac Backus argued, for instance, that while a proper theological education could equip one to be a wiser and more skillful minister of the Word, the "internal call" of the Spirit was an absolute must for true and effective gospel ministry. He stated it this way:

> One very great means that God has been pleased to make use of from the beginning for the recovery and salvation of lost men, has been the preaching of the Word. And therefore in every age he has called and set apart particular men for that purpose. Jude speaks of Enoch's *prophesying*, Jude 14. And Noah is called a *preacher of righteousness*, 2 Pet. 2:5...Hence it is a truth allowed in general by all persuasions, that the public preaching of the Word is an ordinance of divine appointment. But then there is a diversity of sentiments about how men are to be qualified and introduced into this great work. Multitudes place their qualifications more in human learning than in divine enlightening, and place their authority more in being externally called and set apart by men, than in being internally called by the Spirit of God. Yea, many seem to make no account of the latter, but set it aside as an extraordinary thing, not to be expected in these days. And the main argument that is commonly brought to prove this is, that the Bible is completed, and the days of inspiration are ceased; therefore to hold that any are by the Spirit and power of God in these days, called and sent forth into this work, this they say is giving heed to new revelations: for it is nowhere expressed in Scripture that this or that man is, or ever will be, called to preach the Gospel. But though I believe with all my heart that the canon of Scripture is full, and that a curse is denounced against any that shall *add to* or *diminish from it*, Rev. 22:18, 19; yet I am far from thinking that it is just to conclude from hence that the Lord does not in these days as really call and direct his servants by his Spirit as he did in old time; yea, to deny this is to contradict a great part of the Scriptures.[8]

And William Law, while he also did not deny the usefulness of theological education in being a wiser and more skilled communicator of God's Word, further pointed out not only the deadness, but also the real harm of any ministry that relies on any learning devoid of the Spirit's anointing:

> On the basis of a prescribed religious education, the clergyman is

thought to be fully qualified to engage in that ministry for which the apostles had to receive an enduement of power from on high. This scholarly worship of the letter has greatly opposed the ministry of the Holy Spirit, and blinded men to the living reality which the gospel holds out to those who believe...When this empty, powerless knowledge of the letter is held to be the possession of the truth itself, then darkness, delusion, and death overshadow Christendom. For gospel Christianity is in its whole nature a ministration of the Spirit.[9]

Well, perhaps as they say, I have been "preaching to the choir" on this matter of the priority of the Spirit's gifting and for Christian leadership and ministry. And whether any hierarchists are willing to listen and take heed to what has been said, God only knows. However, I again urge that, should there ever be a reconciliation conference between egalitarians and hierarchical-complementarians, the egalitarians refuse to compromise on this matter. Remember and do not forget Paul's word on the difference between ministry under the old and new covenants: "[God] has made us competent as ministers of a new covenant--not of the letter but of the Spirit; for the letter kills, but the Spirit gives life" (2 Cor. 3:6, TNIV).

Endnotes

1. Alister E. McGrath, *Christianity's Dangerous Idea: The Protestant Revolution*, p. 53.

2. Alice P. Mathews, "Toward Reconciliation: Healing the Schism," *Discovering Biblical Equality*, pp. 494-495.

3. William J. Webb, "A Redemptive-Movement Hermeneutic," *Discovering Biblical Equality*, p. 384.

4. At the annual meeting of the Evangelical Theological Society in November 2016, in a session that focused on the Trinity, Wayne Grudem and Bruce Ware stated they no longer held that the eternal generation of the Son was a valid ground for the eternal subordination of the Son.

Though an important shift in their thinking, it comes short of a full acknowledgment and repudiation of the erroneous view of the Trinity that became widespread through their writings.

5. Shirlely Guthrie, "Who Is God?," *Christian Doctrine, Revised Edition*, p.82.

6. Kevin Giles, *Jesus and the Father: Modern Evangelicals Reinvent the Doctrine of the Trinity*; Milliard Erickson, *Who's Tampering With the Trinity?: An Assessment of the Subordination Debate*; Alan Myatt, "On The Compatibility of Ontological Equality, Hierarchy and Functional Distinctions," a theological paper presented at the 61st annual meeting of the Evangelical Theological Society (ETS).

7. Patrick S. Franklin, "Women Sharing in the Ministry of God: A Trinitarian Framework for the Priority of Spirit-Gifting as a Solution to the Gender Debate," *Priscilla Papers*, Vol. 22, No.4, Autumn 2008, p. 14.

8. "A Discourse Showing the Nature and Necessity of An Internal Call to Preach The Everlasting Gospel," *Isaac Backus on Church, State and Calvinism*, p.75.

9. William Law, *An Affectionate Address to the Clergy*, pp.39-41, as quoted by Pam Morrison, "The Holy Spirit, Neglected Person of the Trinity, and Women's Leadership," *Priscilla Papers*, Vol. 22, No.4, Autumn 2008, p.22.

Bibliography

Barnett, Paul. *Is The New Testament History?* Ann Arbor, MI: Vine Books, 1986.

Bock, Darrell. *Luke, NIV Application Commentary.* Grand Rapids, MI: Zondervan, 2009.

Blomberg, Craig. *The Historical Reliability of the Gospels.* Downers Grove, IL: InterVarsity Press, 1987.

———. *The Historical Reliability of John's Gospel.* Downers Grove, IL: InterVarsity Press, 2001.

———. "Who was Jesus? Modern Myths vs. Bible Basics." *Focal Point* (Winter 1996): 15-21.

Bowman Jr., Robert M. *Orthodoxy and Heresy: A Biblical Guide to Doctrinal Discernment.* Grand Rapids, MI: Baker Book House, 1992.

Brown, Raymond E. *An Introduction to New Testament Christology.* New York, NY: Paulist Press, 1994.

Bruce, F.F. *The Books and the Parchments,* rev. ed. Tappan, PA: Flemming Revell, 1985.

Comfort, Philip W., ed. *The Origin of the Bible.* Wheaton, IL: Tyndale, 1992.

Davies, W.D. "The Historicity of Jesus." In *Invitation to the New Testament: A Guide to the Main Witnesses.* Philadelphia, PA: Fortress Press, 1978.

Dunn, J.G. "The Historicity of the Synoptic Gospels." In *Crisis in Christology,* 201-202. Edited by William R. Farmer. Mesquite, TX: Truth Incorporated, 1995.

Edwards, John R. "Who Do Scholars Say That I Am?" *Christianity Today*

40, no.3 (March 4, 1996): 16-19.

Erickson, Millard J. *Who's Tampering With the Trinity? An Assessment of the Subordination Debate.* Grand Rapids, MI: Kregel, 2009.

Evans, Richard J. *In Defense of History.* New York, NY: Norton, 1999.

Franklin, Patrick S. "Women Sharing in the Ministry of God: A Trinitarian Framework for the Priority of Spirit-Gifting as a Solution to the Gender Debate." *Priscilla Papers* 22, no.4 (Autumn 2008): 14-20.

Fee, Gordon. *Listening to the Spirit in the Text.* Grand Rapids, MI: Eerdmans, 2000.

———."Hermeneutics and the Gender Debate."Chap. 21 in *Discovering Biblical Equality: Complimentarity Without Hierarchy.* Edited by Ronald W. Pierce and Rebecca M. Groothuis. Downers Grove, IL: InterVarsity Press, 2005.

———. "The Priority of Spirit Gifting for Church Ministry." Chap. 14 in *Discovering Biblical Equality: Complementarity Without Hierarchy.* Edited by Ronald W. Pierce and Rebecca M. Groothuis. Downers Grove, IL: InterVarsity Press, 2005.

Giles, Kevin. *Jesus and the Father: Modern Evangelicals Reinvent the Doctrine of the Trinity.* Grand Rapids, MI: Zondervan, 2005.

———."Response to the Melbourne Hierarchical-Complementarians." (CBE Free Article, 2010).

Grenz, Stanley. *Theology for the Community of God.* Nashville, TN: Broadman and Holman, 1994.

Guthrie, Shirley C. *Christian Doctrine,* Revised Edition. Louisville, Ky: Westminster John Knox Press, 1994.

Hirsch Jr., E.D. *Validity In Interpretation.* New Haven, CT: Yale University Press, 1978.

Johnson, Luke Timothy. *The Real Jesus: The Misguided Quest for the Historical Jesus and the Truth of the Traditional Gospels.* San Francisco, CA: HarperCollins, 1996.

Johnson, Robert K., ed. *The Use of the Bible in Theology: Evangelical Options.* Atlanta, GA: John Knox Press, 1985.

Kantzer, Kenneth S., ed. *Applying the Scriptures: Papers from ICBI Summit III.* Grand Rapids, MI: Zondervan, 1987.

Keller, Werner. *The Bible As History,* 2nd rev. ed. New York, NY: Barnes and Noble, 1980.

Maier, John P. *Jesus, A Marginalized Jew: Rethinking the Historical Jesus, vol. 1.* New York, NY: Doubleday, 1991.

Martin, Ralph P. *Reconciliation: A Study of Paul's Theology.* Grand Rapids, MI: Zondervan, 1989.

McGrath, Alister. *Christianity's Dangerous Idea: The Protestant Revolution.* New York, NY: HarperCollins, 2007.

———. *Heresy: A History of Defending the Truth.* New York, NY: HarperCollins, 2009.

McLoughlin, William G., ed. *Isaac Backus on Church, State and Calvinism: Pamphlets 1754-1789.* Cambridge, MA: Harvard University Press, 1968.

Milne, Bruce. *Know the Truth: A Handbook of Christian Belief,* rev. ed. Downers Grove, IL: InterVarsity Press, 1998.

Morrison, Pam. "The Holy Spirit, Neglected Person of the Trinity, and Women's Leadership," *Priscilla Papers* 22, no. 4 (Autumn 2008): 21-24.

Myatt, Alan. "On The Compatibility of Ontological Equality, Hierarchy, and Functional Distinctions." Paper presented at the 61st Annual Meeting of the Evangelical Theological Society, November 2010.

Packer, James I. "God the Image-Maker" In *Christian Faith and Practice in the Modern World*. Edited by Mark A. Noll and David F. Wells. Grand Rapids, MI: Eerdmans, 1988.

Radmacher, Earl D. and Robert D. Preus, eds. *Hermeneutics, Inerrancy, and the Bible: Papers from ICBI Summit II*. Grand Rapids, MI: Zondervan, 1984.

Ramm, Bernard. *Protestant Biblical Interpretation: A Textbook of Hermeneutics*, 3rd rev. ed. Grand Rapids, MI: Baker Book House, 1977.

Schroeder, Gerald L. *The Science of God: The convergence of Scientific and Biblical Wisdom*. New York, NY: Free Press, 2008.

Strobel, Lee. *The Case for the Real Jesus: A Journalist Investigates Current Attacks on the Identity of Jesus*. Grand Rapids, MI: Zondervan, 2007.

Swanstrom, Roy. *History In the Making: An Introduction to the Study of the Past*. Downers Grove, IL: InterVarsity Press, 1978.

Swartley, Willard M. *Slavery, Sabbath, War and Women: Case Issues in Biblical Interpretation*. Scottsdale, PA: Herald Press, 1983.

Turrentini, Francis. *The Doctrine of Scripture*. Translated and edited by John W. Beardslee III. Grand Rapids, MI: Baker Book House, 1981.

Wallace, Daniel B. "Inerrancy and the Text of the New Testament." In *Evidence for God: 50 Arguments for Faith from the Bible, History, Science and Philosophy*, 211-219. Edited by William A. Dembski and Michael R. Licona. Grand Rapids, MI: Baker Books, 2006.

Williamson, G.A. "Introduction," *Josephus, The Jewish War: An English Translation*. Baltimore, MD: Penguin Classics, 1960.

Witherington III, Ben. *The Jesus Quest: The Third Search for the Jew of Nazareth*. Downers Grove, IL: InterVarsity Press, 1995.

———. *The Paul Quest: The Renewed Search for the Jew of Tarsus*. Downers Grove, IL: InterVarsity Press, 1998.

Woodbridge, John D. *Biblical Authority: A Critique of the Rogers/McKim Proposal*. Grand Rapids, MI: Zondervan, 1982.

Wright, N.T. *Jesus and the Victory of God: Christian Origins and the Question of God, vol 2*. New York, NY: Fortress Press, 1997.

About Christians for Biblical Equality

Christians for Biblical Equality (CBE) is a nonprofit organization of Christian men and women who believe that the Bible, properly interpreted, teaches the fundamental equality of men and women of all ethnic groups, all economic classes, and all age groups, based on the teachings of Scriptures such as Galatians 3:28:

> "There is neither Jew nor Gentile, neither slave nor free, nor is there male and female, for you are all one in Christ Jesus" (NIV 2011).

Mission Statement

CBE exists to promote biblical justice and community by educating Christians that the Bible calls women and men to share authority equally in service and leadership in the home, church, and world.

Who we are

We are Christians, committed to the Bible. We believe that the Bible is the inspired Word of God, is reliable, and is the final authority for Christian faith and practice. We believe that our mission is a result of faithful interpretation and application of the Bible.

We are a global community. CBE partners, supporters, and organizational members come from over sixty countries and every corner of the United States. They advocate for the shared authority of men and women in their families, churches, workplaces, and cultures all over the world. Together, we make this mission a reality.

We are lifelong learners. We believe that there is always more to learn about God and God's purposes in the world, and God's Word. We provide educational resources on issues pertaining to gender and the Bible for a variety of audiences. We seek to engage with believers of all backgrounds and together sharpen our understanding.

What we do

CBE's ministry revolves around several core components.

Publications. We publish an academic journal, *Priscilla Papers*, and a popular magazine, *Mutuality*, quarterly. These award-winning publications are available by mail with a paid subscription or for free on CBE's website. Audio and video recordings from CBE conferences are also accessible for free through our website. In addition, we publish a blog with a weekly e-newsletter, *Arise*.

Bookstore. CBE Bookstore is the place to find the best resources on the biblical perspective on the equal service and authority of men and women. Each book we carry or recommend has been reviewed for quality and relevance to CBE's mission. To find egalitarian books, visit cbebookstore.org.

Conferences. Each year, we host an international conference with some of the top scholars and speakers in the world. Our conferences educate, encourage, and equip our community to share about the biblical basis for the shared authority of men and women in their homes, churches, and cultures.

Organizational Membership. Whether your church or organization is exploring biblical equality or is already committed to it, CBE membership provides you with resources and support. CBE organizational membes receive free subscriptions to our publications, discounts at CBE Bookstore, and conference registration discounts, as well as other benefits.

Chapters. Chapters are CBE's hands and feet in communities around the world. Chapters are a way for local CBE members and supporters to connect and minister together. They often host lectures, meet for mutual encouragement, represent CBE at regional conferences, and serve their communities together.

Core Values

- Scripture is our authoritative guide for faith, life, and practice.
- Patriarchy (male dominance) is not a biblical ideal but a result of sin.
- Patriarchy is an abuse of power, taking from females what God has given them: their dignity, and freedom, their leadership, and often their very lives.
- While the Bible reflects patriarchal culture, the Bible does not teach patriarchy in human relationships.
- Christ's redemptive work frees all people from patriarchy, calling women and men to share authority equally in service and leadership.
- God's design for relationships includes faithful marriage between a man and a woman, celibate singleness and mutual submission in Christian community.
- The unrestricted use of women's gifts is integral to the work of the Holy Spirit and essential for the advancement of the gospel in the world.
- Followers of Christ are to oppose injustice and patriarchal teachings and practices that marginalize and abuse females and males.

Envisioned Future

CBE envisions a future where all believers are freed to exercise their gifts for God's glory and purposes, with the full support of their Christian communities.

www.ingramcontent.com/pod-product-compliance
Lightning Source LLC
Chambersburg PA
CBHW061340040426
42444CB00011B/3012